The Spirit Within

Insights from the Autism Spectrum

Shay McAtee, MA, OTR/L

Publishing Partners
Port Townsend, WA
books@publishing-partners.com
www.marciabreece.com

Cover image: "The Artist" Amberly, page 168

Printed in the United States of America

Library of Congress Control Number: 2019935853

ISBN 978-1-944887414

Photography: Shay McAtee
Graphic Designer: Judy Robertson
Book production: Marcia Breece

— CONTENTS —

— DEDICATION —

To the parents and their children who said "yes" when asked to share
their autism spectrum experience. They made this book possible.

— INTRODUCTION —

Autism can affect the way a person interprets and interacts within the world around them. It can also affect the ability of those unfamiliar with the diagnosis to understand and connect with these complex individuals. This project emerged from a long-held desire to help us all better understand those on the autism spectrum. I approached each session fully appreciating how much I had to learn about how these individuals and families functioned on a day by day, hour by hour basis, outside of school and clinic settings. While my experience as an occupational therapist positioned me to be interested in what they had to teach me, it is the parents who are the true experts.

The sessions took place in the family's home or in another familiar location, usually beginning with the interview, allowing time for the child or teen to get used to my presence. Beyond that it was an organic process, moving between interviewing and photography, occasionally doing both at the same time. I knew that I wasn't experiencing the full range of life with these individuals, but in the two to three hour sessions I was given a glimpse of who they were within the matrix of their family.

I was impressed by how each family adapted their rhythms and routines to the personality of their particular child. There was flexibility and a heightened ability to anticipate the child's practical and emotional needs. In the best moments it was like a dance, the flow of the family around their child, and the child within the family. In the middle of one interview, the father stood up and, while still talking, spread a beach towel across the tracks of the sliding glass door. He paused and said, "It's going to get wet here," sat back down and continued with his story. Moments later his son came in from the yard, empty sand bucket in hand, filled the bucket with water, headed back outside, and tripped on the door track, spilling some water.

When photographing, I followed the child's lead. One 3-year-old boy playfully ducked under his bed, so I followed and photographed him there. In some cases the child chose to pose, while others ignored the camera, continuing with whatever activity engaged them. I was more interested in entering the child's world and finding the photos there, than setting up a specific shot.

There was a boy I was scheduled to photograph who met me at the front door, a smile spreading across his face, as if to say, "You're here! You're at my house." I knew this boy from the clinic where I was a supervisor. He had been having a difficult time and I would often help when he was upset. I expected a more fragile child. Instead, here was a grinning boy, in his element, bringing me into the living room, taking my hands, and leading me in a dance. His mother smiled and said, "He's happy to see you." This almost completely non-verbal child was clearly highly communicative, inviting me into his world.

On another visit, the boy I was to photograph had just arrived home from school. I followed him outside as he played, spinning and running in circles, jumping from a bench pretending to fly, playing with a hula hoop, and climbing the monkey bars. As I watched and photographed, it became clear that he wasn't randomly moving from one thing to the next. This often non-verbal child was showing me his favorite after-school activities. I started noticing the little pauses as he decided what he wanted to show me next, and the quick glance and smile in my direction before he took off again. He was showing me what brought him joy. I thought I was the initiator, but he was the one leading the conversation.

Ryan, a 6-year-old boy with autism and limited speech, had just finished his OT session. He was ready to go home, but his mother and I were still talking. He was unhappy and began lightly tossing toy blocks against the wall. I started tossing blocks with him, acknowledging his frustration. Ryan stopped, looked up at me, and smiled. His mother said, "He so loves it when someone gets him." My intention is for this project to help us all better understand Ryan and other individuals on the autism spectrum.

– Shay McAtee

DAMIEN - 5 YEARS | 2 MONTHS, with his mom and baby sister

— THREE TO FIVE YEARS —

I think that every parent is devastated when they first get the diagnosis. It feels like it's the end of the world. But it's important for parents who have a new diagnosis to know that it's not the end of the world. There is a light at the end of the tunnel. You need to get early treatment for your child. And you need to get a really good support group for yourself. That was important for me.

– *Cami's mom*

Every day is not a great day, but every day is not a terrible day either. Now I look at Stephen and I'm more at peace with his autism. It's been two years since he got diagnosed, and we do what we can from day to day. As long as he's happy, it's good.

– *Stephen's mom*

As long as Ryan is prepped, he does pretty well. There aren't as many anxiety issues now. He looks forward to the bus coming down the street. Fortunately, the school district has been pretty easy to work with, accommodating, and helpful in getting us what we needed. It's being able to envision the long-term benefit. You have to keep trying.

– *Ryan's dad*

There's a lot of ignorance out there about autism. When I talk to people, they often say, "Oh, I thought that once you're autistic, your life is just doomed. That's it." And I tell them, "No. There's hope for these kids. There are different therapies and they can become much more integrated in society. They can emerge."

– *Annabella's mom*

— KYLE —

3 YEARS | 8 MONTHS

With autism, it's a lot of little success stories.

Kyle's dad

Like when Kyle started recognizing emotion in someone else.
Now he'll say, "Mommy, you're sad. I'll make it better," and give
me a hug. That is amazing coming from him.

Kyle's mom

– KYLE –

How would you describe Kyle's personality?

MOM: Kyle is very tied into his emotions. He just explodes with emotions. That can be good or it can be bad. He has the most infectious laughter, and his sense of humor is wonderful now that he has it back. He was that way originally, but then we lost him for a long time. When his humor started coming back we were so happy. We had him back. He's a lot more conversational now that he has speech[1]. He will talk your ear off. Kyle has Pervasive Developmental Disorder Not Otherwise Specified (PDDNOS). Early intervention has also really helped Kyle improve.

DAD: He has his moments though.

MOM: There are some days that are really bad and full of sensory issues. And there are days that are just perfect and sublime and I get compliments from people about how well behaved Kyle and Ryan[2] are. I'm thinking to myself, "If you only knew what we went through."

DAD: We have therapies, we have playgroups, especially during the summer it's just go, go, go.

MOM: Because if we don't, we see regression. We have to maintain stability with our scheduling, because otherwise it's just chaos all the time and I go crazy. But we've got the diet pretty much under control and they're really well tempered now.

We really resisted putting Kyle and Ryan on a special diet. We didn't want to do it. We were dead set against it. Finally, after getting so much information from so many different people, and reading voraciously, we decided to try it over the summer break. Two weeks later Kyle started talking.

With both the kids, we've had to do a lot of thinking, "Okay, what are we concerned about? What are their strengths? What are their weaknesses?" I'd literally write down lists of everything and we'd talk about it. We'd talk with their different therapists about the issues that they see as well. We also participated in research projects and thesis projects; whatever we could find.

---

1   Speech: speech and language therapy

2   Ryan, page 42

How is it when you are out in the community?

MOM: There was a point when I couldn't take Kyle out in public, because I knew it would be torture. I used to feel people's eyes on me thinking that I was such a bad mom, that I couldn't even manage my children. The boys weren't doing it on purpose. There was always a cloud over us whenever we went out. So I would try to run out by myself. I would never, ever bring the boys out in public, unless I had someone else with me. Every time I tried taking them out on my own I ended up crying, because it was so hard. I'd wait until their father got home from work to help me with the kids while I furiously shopped. Or I'd have a friend come with me. I have some very supportive friends. That was the only way I could do it.

When we were starting to understand what was going on, our occupational therapist actually met me at the grocery store and taught me ways to get through shopping with Kyle. She also met me at the library to help us understand why he'd scream his head off whenever we went there. Now I understand why he would cover his ears. Now I understand a lot more and I can read him better. I can anticipate things so that they don't come to a head. If I took a different route to a familiar destination he would start screaming like he was being burned or something. He would throw toys at my head. It was getting dangerous to drive with him. It's a lot less stressful going out into the public now.

We were worried about our first trip on an airplane because Kyle has such sensitive ears. Also, he doesn't like being confined. We went to the closest destination that we could find. We wanted to try them on an airplane. It had to be close to home. We didn't want anything more than two and a half hours or so.

We had their grandmother with us, so Grandy and I tag-teamed Kyle, and Dad sat with Ryan. Going there really wasn't all that bad. It was coming back that was bad for Kyle because he was distracted and bored and he didn't get to do what he wanted, which is hard for him. We all had on autism t-shirts. Kyle's said, "Beware of autism meltdown." Ryan's had a little face that said,

"What? Is my autism showing?" Mine said, "I asked God for a blessing and he gave me my two autistic sons." Dad had on his autism shirt and Grandy had on her shirt. Luckily we didn't really have any major melt-downs, but just in case we wanted people to know. Even though the way home was more difficult, it was still doable. Kyle wasn't screaming for two and a half hours. He had a number of games to keep him busy. We got headphones for each of them so they could listen to their games. The headphones also helped with the compression of their ears. Kyle wears sunglasses, a baseball cap, and earmuffs to go anywhere. It helps mediate light and noise, and helps him feel more contained and enclosed.

Do you have a favorite story about Kyle?

DAD: With autism, it's a lot of little success stories.

MOM: Like when Kyle started recognizing emotion in someone else. Now he'll say, "Mommy, you're sad. I'll make it better," and give me a hug. That is amazing coming from him. And of course I'll start sobbing. It was also exciting when he started showing more imaginative play. Having him go through a story with me where he's making up stuff on his own was so wonderful!

Our neighbors can let their kids frolic in the neighborhood and play at neighbors houses. We can't let our kids do that, because I can't guarantee that they would understand the boundaries. Our neighbors, they would never consider not doing it, because their kids have a concept of personal safety and boundaries. Our kids don't. You appreciate the small things more than parents with typical kids might. For a typical kid it might be something small. But for us it's huge. It's just little stupid stuff for typical kids, but for us it's big!

— VICTOR —

3 YEARS | 8 MONTHS

When Victor wakes up he crawls into my bed and starts jabbering
away. Sometimes it makes me cry because I can't understand him.
But mostly I'm just saying, "Really?"
I just wish I could understand what he's telling me.

Victor's mom

I understand that your twins are both on the spectrum. How would you describe Victor?

MOM: I call Victor, and his twin brother Efren[3], "my monkeys." They are always climbing on and jumping off things. Victor can jump from one piece of furniture to the couch, three feet away, and land on his bottom in a sitting position. He's amazing.

Victor is funny. He used to talk to his "Woody" doll. He would say something to him and then hold Woody up to his ear expecting Woody to reply. But Woody was broken. So my mom bought him a new Woody that would actually work. Once Woody started talking, Victor never talked to him again.

Victor is a little more social than Efren. He doesn't have too much of a problem with people getting near him and holding him. You tickle him and he's yours. That's all it takes for him to love you. He's just very silly.

When Victor wakes up he crawls into my bed and starts jabbering away. Sometimes it makes me cry because I can't understand him. But mostly I'm just saying, "Really?" I just wish I could understand what he's telling me. He's probably saying, "Mom, I dreamt about this," or, "I did this in my dream." Who knows? But he wakes up, gets into my bed, and cuddles up. He'll get under the covers and start jabbering away.

Victor used to eat dirt. They both did, but more Victor. I tried so many different things to get him to stop eating dirt. Finally, I found that powdered chocolate milk has a little bit of the same texture and same color. It's not great. It's sugar. But at least it's not dirt. And, it satisfies whatever sensory needs he has. Most important, he stopped eating dirt.

Does he tend to seek sensory experiences or avoid them?

MOM: Victor seeks a lot of sensory input. He's always putting things in his mouth. He'll put a rock in his mouth and just swish it around. I think it has to do with texture. I think that's what the dirt was about.

---

3   Efren, page 10

– VICTOR –

Also, he likes certain sounds. He'll gather a bunch of pebbles and throw them in the air. I think he likes the sound of them hitting the ground. He does the same thing with water. He'll throw water up and when it splashes on the floor, he just giggles uncontrollably.

He loves deep pressure. He's good at giving big hugs. He does avoid a few things, like certain paints. He's fine if they're around, but once he gets them on him, he kind of freaks out. He loves deep pressure massages. He'll zone out sometimes with the deep pressure. Victor always has a little stick or little toy in his hand. I think that's kind of like his security blanket. He usually has something in his hand. He also likes to collect shiny things. Victor is my crow.

Victor will give you kisses, which is really his way of saying, "I want something. Please!" And it's usually something that he knows he's not supposed to have, like more chocolate. He's also always looking for the physical. The more physical something is and the more deep pressure and heavy work, the better. He likes hugs and climbing and hanging upside down.

For Victor his food has to be very bland. He is a chicken nugget boy. That's his steak. He eats chicken nuggets and rice. If I want him to get more protein, I'll grill meat outside. He loves that. But it has to be meat that's been cooked outside on the grill.

How are the boys when you're out in the community? And how are people in the community with your boys?

MOM: A lot of the time people don't believe me when I tell them that the boys have autism. We went to a friend's birthday party. Victor, of course, had his stick in his hand. He was in the living room, swinging it around. This little old lady grabbed the stick from him and he, of course, started crying. I told her, "These are my kids. What's going on?" She said that Victor was trying to hit all the other kids and that he's not playing nice. I said, "That's not what he's doing. The stick is his security. He feels better when he has that stick in his hand." It wasn't dangerous and pointy or anything. But she did not believe me when I told her about him. She said, "Your kids aren't disabled!" And, I said, "Yes, they are. They have autism. They're not physically disabled. You can't see it. But they don't understand. When you take the stick away from him just like that, he doesn't understand."

To be honest, when we're out in the community, I do feel embarrassed sometimes. But I always think about them. I would rather go through the embarrassment, than have them locked up at home. In the long run, it's going to help them because they're going to be exposed to the world and not be hermits. I do it for them. We go to the park two to three times a week. And once a week we do something big. We might go to the outdoor swap meet where it's really crowded. Or we go to the mall. My dad has a rodeo and a lot of people come with horses. There's a lot of traffic. But we do things like that to get them exposed to it.

It can be rough being with them out in the community. Victor thinks it's funny to get away from someone. That's his thing. It's the chase. He'll run, giggling and laughing, but not knowing if anyone is actually following him. That's the danger. He wants to take off. It's his little game. He thinks it's hilarious. With Victor every thing is a game. He's so silly.

Do you ever try to imagine what is going on in his head.
MOM: Yes. One day he was lying on the ground looking under the truck staring at who knows what. I went over and laid down as well, trying to figure out what he was looking at. Maybe he was looking at the rocks, maybe the little tiny holes in the rocks or the different colors. Who knows? But I was just trying to get into his zone. It takes a lot of imagination.

Maybe it's like being on different planets?
MOM: Yes. And, we're trying to build a bridge to get over there.

— EFREN —

3 YEARS | 8 MONTHS

Efren stays to himself. It takes him longer to adjust to
someone new. He will just ignore people
until he feels comfortable.

Efren's mom

How would you describe Efren?

MOM: Efren has more of a temper than his twin brother Victor[4]. He used to tantrum for thirty minutes to almost an hour at times. He would hit us and bang things. It was just horrible. I think it had more to do with his inability to communicate. He didn't know how to tell us what was wrong or what he felt. Once he started a tantrum he couldn't stop. He would throw the chairs. He's broken a couple of chairs. We had to keep their older and younger brothers away so he wouldn't hit them. It's getting a lot better since they went to the occupational therapy clinic. He's calmed down a lot. He does still tantrum occasionally, but not as much.

Efren is my grouchy one. He is also very determined. If he wants to do something, he's very determined to do it. He's been practicing on his tricycle. He's so determined to learn how to ride a tricycle. He's been scooting himself on it for a while, but the other day, for the first time, he actually peddled for about ten feet. He's that determined with everything. If I give him a puzzle, he gets very upset if someone tries to help him. If I put a piece in, he get mad and takes it out. He has to do it himself. He is very determined to do it himself and to learn how to do it himself.

Efren stays to himself. It takes him longer to adjust to someone new. He will just ignore people until he feels comfortable. It takes him more time. Efren wants to cuddle with me at night. He doesn't want me to hold him, but he wants me next to him. He's really funny. He wants to feel me next to him, but he doesn't want me to hug him.

Efren and Victor both pretty much ignore other kids and stay to themselves, unless they see something that another child has that they want. Then it's "toddler rules." They will actually try to interact with the other child, but basically they're just trying to get the toy. Once they do, they'll go off and do their own thing again.

Efren is very sensitive to sounds. If their little brother screams too much he will go after him. If I yell at all, he'll let me know, "Stop. Be quiet. Don't do that." Sounds that have a certain pitch really bother him. I took him to the grocery store once. We just walked in and he covered his ears and freaked out. I think it was the pitch or tone of the overhead announcements.

---

4   Victor, page 6

— EFREN —

Efren has more of a range of what he'll eat than Victor. He loves pepperoni. He loves burritos. He loves bread. He loves apples and oranges and grapes. It's not very many things but it's a range. He'll sometimes eat rice. He likes spicy stuff for some reason.

How does Efren communicate?

MOM: He doesn't really have much language. He won't come up to me and say, "Hey, I want this." I think they both say a lot more but we're just not understanding them because it's not very clear yet. They are both better now at indicating what they want. Before, it was just crying and hitting. I couldn't figure out what they wanted. "Are you hungry? Are you thirsty? Are you in pain?" It was very hard. I would bring something to Efren to see if that's what he wanted and he would tantrum because he couldn't communicate and I didn't know what he wanted. I would take him around the house to see if I could figure out what he wanted. I think they both finally got the point. Now they'll take me to what they want. When Efren is watching a familiar video he'll repeat everything as it is being said on the TV, but he doesn't repeat it or use it later.

Professionals might call them severely involved because of their lack of language. To me, they are higher functioning. They're able to communicate in other ways. At home, they are in their own environment and they know how to get things they want. If I were to drop them off at a daycare and nobody knew them, then yes, they would be considered severely involved. But, give them a couple of months there and I don't believe they'll be the same kids that walked in on the first day.

They have surprised me, each of them, in their own way. I had Efren at the doctor's for his physical. He was very upset about being undressed. He was crying and screaming during the exam. I finally got him dressed and he started tapping me, saying "Dad. Dad." I said, "You want to go with Dad? Okay. That's awesome that you're telling me, that you're talking to me. We'll go with Dad right now." But I was still talking to the doctor and he pulled me and he said, "Ma, 's go now!" I was amazed. That was a whole sentence! That was about a month ago and I haven't heard it again.

People think that kids with autism are not loving. At first they didn't seem to be connected. I would try to hug them and they would push me away and scream. It was like it hurt them. Eventually, they allowed me to hug them, but they weren't hugging back. Finally, now, they will hug me. They will come to me for a hug. They will ask for affection. Now I think the connection is there. I know they have loved me from the very beginning. But maybe they showed it in a different way which I didn't understand. Maybe by pushing me they were saying, "Hey, Mom. I love you," and I just didn't understand. But I showed them that they could show me by hugging and it just clicked in. They are changing.

With autism, it's important to know that every kid is different. Saying a kid has autism doesn't tell you everything. Every kid is on a different level and learns at a different pace. They see things in a different way than we will ever be able to see.

— ROMAN —

4 YEARS | 1 MONTH

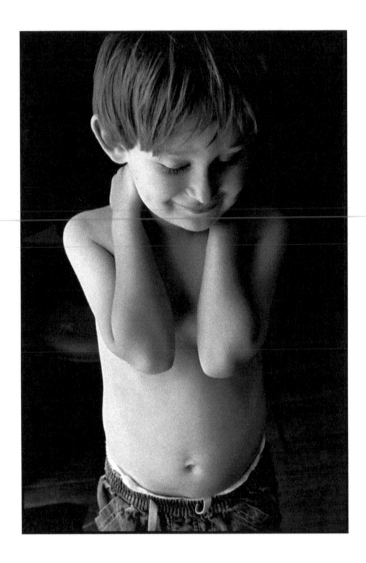

Roman's qualities are wonderful, and good, and I accept that and love that. But you don't know if others will as well. You just hope that there's a place in the world for him that accepts him.

Roman's mom

– ROMAN –

How would you describe Roman?

MOM: It's a little tough to describe Roman because he's babyish as compared to typically developing kids. He's somewhat curious about the physical world and he loves music. It's fortunate for us that he is physically loving and responsive, despite his condition. You want to be able to interact with your child in a way that is good for them and rewarding for you. I think that is key. The fact that he will come to us, touch us, and let us kiss him and hold him, and that he likes physical squishes and hugs is really important to us. I'm so grateful that he is like that. I'm so grateful that he isn't shut in more. I'm grateful that he does have some words and that he has this spark about him. In the end you accept, love, and help the child that you're given.

Sometimes he does little things that would be typical, if he were two years old. Communication is keeping him back. I think that, even if he could catch up in his language and all those other skills you hope he will develop, he's always going to have a certain innocence or naivety about him. He's going to have the opposite of sophistication. Because typical little kids are picking stuff up from the beginning. They're learning so much, and it accumulates. There's this big part of the foundation that he's not getting. With typical kids that information and those experiences get built upon. For him, there is a gap where he's missing the social subtleties and nuances. So, no matter what, he's already missed out on a lot of that learning.

He doesn't really have any friends because interacting with him is hard work. I get it. He's work, and not that many people know how to interact with him. The people who do work with him, the people who choose to work with children like Roman as a profession, they're the ones who appreciate him the most. They have the ability to see beyond the disability. They get the person. They're okay with him. But, other people aren't always interested in slowing down. Roman's qualities are wonderful, and good, and I accept that and love that. But you don't know if others will as well. You just hope that there's a place in the world for him that accepts him.

They tell me he's a little bit on the under-aroused side. I guess I'd rather have him be under-aroused than over-aroused. He does like sensory input. He used to bang on his head or bang his head against me. We worked with him to give him more appropriate sensory input, like squeezes, and hugs, and squishes with pillows. We also have a little trampoline and a lycra swing. That behavior is not that extreme anymore. He only occasionally hits his head now, but it's not terrible. He comes across as kind of calm, which is maybe his under-arousal state.

How old was he when he received the diagnosis?
MOM: He was two and eight months. By the time we got the diagnosis we weren't shocked. We were sort of expecting it. But still you're really depressed for a while. You have to completely change your expectations. That's true for anyone whose child has any condition. The first week after we received Roman's diagnosis, there was grief. And then there was hope. They had all those services for him.

After about a year I had grief again, because the initial expectation was that all of this progress was going to happen. We were told that he was bright. Maybe the psychologist was trying to make us feel better. As a rule, I don't think psychologists should say things like that. We were expecting a lot. And then what we saw was him lose all his language. So, after a year, I remember feeling depressed again and really worried about him.

My mantra became "we don't know." I can't grieve and I can't really hope for too much. We just don't know. We can work and get him everything that we can. We can push for services. You do just live from moment to moment. Some are good, some are hard, and some are just calm. But ultimately we can't help but bond with our children and want to do anything we can to help them.

It is a little bit sad that as soon as you're given a disabled child, you're put in a different category. For a long time we didn't need to tell anybody that he was autistic. He was so little, and you don't expect kids to be socialized when they're three. Now, I wish that I could tell people in a way without saying "autism." But it's the shortcut to telling people that this person has a disability and to not expect the same things from him. They usually don't necessarily know about autism, but I tell them that if they want to know anything I'll answer their questions. I have mixed feelings about going out announcing it to the world. But I also suppose that if I were a part of the general public, I would appreciate it. It's a way of giving people more of a break.

It sounds like there is a lot to make your way through.
MOM: There is a lot of information. That's been really hard. You don't want to miss anything that might help. But I'm a skeptic. I want to be rational. Sometimes I step back and think about how we are all just this big huge group of humanity. We're all trying to figure out this stuff. We're like a big tribe, saying "This week we figured out this. Now we know this. Try this. Try that." It's a lot like the game of "telephone." The message can get mixed up. There are a lot of minds and a lot of ideas. There is a lot of information being shared and exchanged. We make a lot of progress, because there are a lot of brains working on it. But there's also a lot that's misunderstood. Eventually we do take a step forward. It is really wonderful that the world is putting so much into the autism issue. But also it's a sad thing that we need to do it.

— E.J. —

4 YEARS | 6 MONTHS

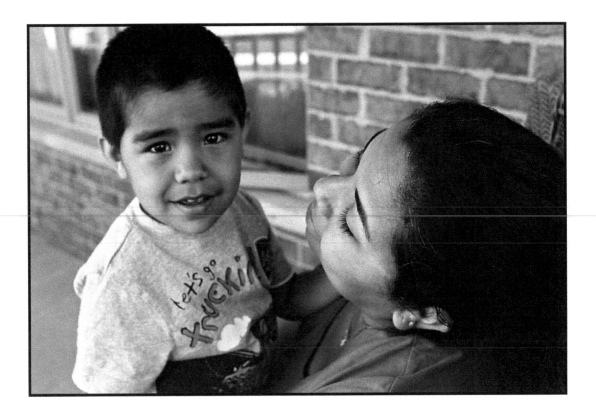

E.J. has a different way of looking at the world than we do. If you think about it, everybody has a different way of looking at the world. It's just that his way of looking at the world doesn't coincide with the rest of society.

E.J.'s mom

— E.J. —

How would you describe E.J.?

MOM: E.J. loves animals. He's always asking to go to the zoo. It seems that a lot of kids with autism really enjoy the simple things, like nature and animals, and are not so much into the materialistic. He likes being outside. He likes going for walks. Now that he has better strength he's a little monkey, climbing things and hanging on things. He loves going to the playground, climbing, swinging and going down the slide. He likes riding his little bike with training wheels.

He's always asking to go somewhere or do something. When we go out, I bring toys that he likes, to keep him occupied. We take pop tubes or a squishy ball or a ball that lights up or a frog toy that he can squish. It helps keep him occupied. He has a whole sensory diet. During the day I try to keep him busy. At home he'll help carry the laundry basket or empty the waste baskets. He's very strong and he likes carrying heavy things. He also likes squeezes and massages. The school district has been absolutely wonderful. They're right on top of it. They have a swing and a trampoline for him.

What else does he enjoy? And are there things he avoids?

MOM: There are sounds that really bother him. He is also sensitive to some tactile things, like tags on his shirts. He's most comfortable in cotton clothes, shirts, pants. Anything else and he starts squirming around. He won't walk barefoot on rocks or on grass.

He also loves hugging the dogs, although they run away from him. He's very affectionate with animals, with his family, and with people he knows or sees a lot. He's more hesitant with family members that he doesn't see a lot. They'll give him a kiss and he wipes his mouth right after. But, they understand. He's a pretty happy kid these days.

Every day it's something new with him. You never know what to expect. He likes building with Legos with his grandpa. He'll play with playdoh with me. He's very curious and wants to find out how things work and what is going on. And he can be quite a jokester. He loves dancing. If a show with dancing is on the TV, he'll grab my hand and try to do the turns. He'll say "Mommy, let's dance." He'll watch the TV and look at their feet and look at their arms and he'll try to copy them.

Right now we have deadbolts on the tops of the doors because he wants to go to the swing set next door. He'll take off and we'll see him next door by himself. The neighbor is great. She watches out for him. The other day I caught him trying to get out. First he brought the chair over, but it wasn't high enough. Then he moved the trampoline over and started jumping, trying to get high enough to get to the dead bolt.

E.J. is very high-functioning. It's because of all the therapies he's had. We have been working with him since he was eighteen months, maybe even before. He started with speech therapy and eventually received occupational and physical therapy. He's also gone to a music class since he was eighteen months. It has really helped. He loves music and it helps him to verbalize. I've had him in speech, OT[5] and PT[6] and in music class since he was eighteen months old.

He started with early intervention, so he's been in school since he was three. He'll be in preschool for one more year and then he'll start kindergarten. That is fine because he is still working on his language and social skills. I'm also trying to potty-train him. He's doing really well.

He desperately wants to play with kids. But he doesn't know how to. He ends up following them or mimicking them, like parallel play. They'll go up the ladder and he'll go up the ladder. They'll go on the slide and he'll go on the slide. He looks for kids. Recently three boys, who were probably eight or nine years old, rode by on their bikes. He said "Hey guys! Wait for me." He didn't know them from Adam.

Considering his diagnosis, he does remarkably well when we're out in the community. He does occasionally act up and people probably think he's being a brat. It's hard if it's the end of the day and he's tired and we have to go to the store. It really changes what we can do. We can't go to

---

5   OT: occupational therapy (or Occupational Therapist)
6   PT: physical therapy (or Physical Therapist)

a restaurant with a live band. I've never had anybody come up and say something to me out in public, but I've seen people look like "what's his problem?" I used to be very concerned about what other people thought, but now I don't care. I can't care. They can make all the faces they want and I just think, "Whatever." It's rough because it's not my job to educate the world. I'm just trying to live my life and keep him happy. But on the other hand, it does seem like when people understand they are more flexible with him.

People can sometimes make assumptions. If someone knew that your son has autism but had not met him, what would you like them to know about E.J.?

MOM: E.J. is just a happy child that has some quirks. He's a normal happy child that has a little difficulty navigating through this world. When you get to know him, he's a beautiful person. E.J. has a different way of looking at the world than we do. If you think about it, everybody has a different way of looking at the world. It's just that his way of looking at the world doesn't coincide with the rest of society. One of my fears is that as the years go by he'll lose his happiness. But I think not. I teach him that everybody is different and some people might be not so nice. But it's okay, because for every mean person there is going to be a really nice person who will be good to him.

— LEORA —
4 YEARS | 7 MONTHS

Leora can understand a lot more than she can say. We seem to
understand each other. It's nice... It's a journey that you can't predict.
You take it one day at a time.
Leora's mom

How would you describe Leora?

MOM: Leora is very loving and sweet. She is always happy. She's not afraid of much, except for loud noises. She's mostly very trusting. She's very loving with adults and she's close to her older brother.

She has trouble with her speech and language. Certain words are clearer. Even though she might not be saying them the right way, I know what she wants. Her understanding has been improving a lot. Leora can understand a lot more than she can say. We seem to understand each other. It's nice. Like if she wants to go to bed, then she will just take me by the hand.

How is she with other kids?

MOM: Right now she doesn't appear to be interested in her peers at school. During recess she mostly plays by herself in the sand.

What does she like to do?

MOM: At school she loves the swings and the slide. At home she likes to play catch. She has a hard time throwing, but she's very good at catching. She started riding her bike with training wheels about two months ago. We were so surprised. She has a lot of problems with her motor skills. My husband had been practicing with her for a long time. We thought that she'd never be able to ride a bike. And then she just started riding it. We were shocked. She does things on her own time. In some ways it makes life more enjoyable. You think, "Okay God, what's next? What is the next step that she's going to achieve?" That's the good part. You don't know. It's always a surprise.

What skills is she developing?

MOM: When she was two and a half she started getting therapy at home. They would try to get her to play with her dolls, but she would just throw them. She wouldn't play with toys the way she should. She would turn the stroller upside down and spin the wheels. Now, she likes her baby dolls. She'll feed her baby, give her baby kisses, and she knows to give them their pacifier. She pushes the doll in the stroller. If the baby doll cries, she pats the baby on the back. It's amazing how far she's come. I used to cry a lot, because she would just throw her toys. She didn't know what to do with them. Now she knows how to play with her dolls. That's a lot. I see a great change.

How was it going from the diagnoses to now?

MOM: When we first got the diagnosis we had no idea about autism. It was hard getting the diagnosis. I was so depressed. It was around the time that we found out that my husband had cancer. It was the worst time of my life. I didn't want to accept her diagnosis. I was thinking, "We won't be able to do our nails together. Will she ever date? Will she ever have a boyfriend? Will she ever get married?" All of those things cross your mind.

I had to let go of all of that and just look at her. Because if all you do is look at autism, the disability, the sad part of it, you'll go under. What is there to like about it? But when you look at her, you see God. You see love. You see joy. She is a blessing. At first it was very hard to accept. My family, my husband's family, and my close friends said, "It's okay. We will love her."

I'm very accepting of her now. But at first I wasn't. It was hard when my girlfriends would talk about their babies or their grandchildren. They would talk about how the child said their first word. It would break my heart, because I'd think, "My daughter is not talking." And I would see little girls taking dancing and swimming classes. Then I'd look at her and all I could say is, "She's going to therapy." I'm still growing. It's getting better. The bottom line is that she's very loving and very loved. She's happy and she brings joy.

I wish there was some kind of way that you could know earlier, but there isn't. As soon as she got diagnosed they let us know that there were services for her. She gets speech, OT, and PT at school. She's also in a behavioral program at school. I'm very happy with all her therapies. The help that's available is amazing. To know that there are people out there to help her brings us joy and peace. Families get so much joy from the help they're receiving.

It sounds like you are really tuned into each other.

MOM: She has made me a better person today. I'm more aware now when I see people with special needs. I'm more aware of the need to make our world more suitable for the handicap. It's a journey that you can't predict. You take it one day at a time. Having her has changed my life in a good way.

— STEPHEN —

4 YEARS | 8 MONTHS

There's this main road that we're paving, and then all these side roads keep opening up.
We've met people who are doing wonderful things for kids with autism...
There's this big puzzle and we're putting in the pieces, one at a time.

Stephen's mom

What would you like to tell me about Stephen?

MOM: Stephen lost his language just before he turned two years old. Up until then he was fully functional, with no signs of autism at all. Then he got sick and he stopped talking. He started pacing. He would pace from the front door to the back door constantly. He wouldn't play with toys. He wouldn't answer when we called his name. He had no eye contact. He started waking up at night screaming or laughing. Sometimes he would be awake at night for two hours straight, just laughing and laughing.

We finally took him to a doctor who specialized in autism. She found vitamin deficiencies and a metal metabolism disorder. He takes in the metals from the environment and can't excrete them like you or I. He had a lot of gastrointestinal problems. Not all kids with autism have gastrointestinal issues like Stephen, but his testing showed that he did. There was something underlying that was causing him to not be able to pay attention and not be able to follow directions. He wasn't able to process information correctly. We changed what he ate and drank, and put him on supplements. He's been gluten free for about two years. He has started sleeping through the night. His eye contact has come back. The pacing completely stopped. He used to stim[7] a lot. When he started the special diet and the biomedical approach, most of his stimming went away. Now he is a little more organized. There are days where Stephen looks phenomenal. Then there are days when he doesn't. Everybody has bad days.

If someone heard that your son has autism, considering the possible assumptions, what would you want them to know about Stephen?

MOM: Stephen is very loving. He has feelings just like you and I. He can hear and understand exactly what we are saying. He has problems expressing himself, but his receptive language is very good. He can do just about everything other children can do, except that at times he needs some modifications. If I tell him to clean up something, he won't do it. But if I say, "Put it in" and I show him by putting a block in, he gets it and can do it all. He needs a more detailed explanation and some modification for certain things.

---

7   Stim or stimming: self-stimulatory repetitive sensory behaviors, such as hand flapping or rocking

— STEPHEN —

He's a good-natured child. Most of the time, he's very easy going. He's a gentle soul. He's happiest when he's moving. He loves swinging, swimming, bike riding, amusement park rides, going up and down the slides at the park. He likes to be free to do what he likes to do. He loves being in the water. He always wants to be moving. That's okay. That's what he wants to do.

He likes to watch kid's language videos. If he wants a little downtime, he'll go out to the backyard. He likes cars, because they move and he likes the wheels. We take him go-karting and he really enjoys it. The thing that I don't ever want him to lose is the joy that he finds in simple things. He likes looking at things in the grass. He likes picking up sticks and putting them through the hole in the swing set. He likes simple things. He loves getting into the pool. His face lights up with joy on an amusement park ride or just riding his bike. He's so free. He's so happy and excited.

What services is he getting?

MOM: We have been using Dr. Greenspan's DIR/Floortime[8] approach with Stephen. We don't do ABA[9]. A lot of people have had success with ABA. It just didn't fit for our son. With the DIR/Floortime approach we first look at what interests Stephen, what motivates him. We let him get regulated, then we engage with him, and work to get the back and forth circles going. If he's motivated by the cars, we'll work on "up and down," "over and under," "stop and go," "one, two, three, go," and "ready, set, go." There are so many opportunities day in and day out. Once a month we travel ninety minutes one way to see an OT that has a DIR/Floortime program.

Stephen is also getting OT in a clinic with swings and things. They use a sensory integration approach. He has an abundance of sensory issues. He's a sensory seeker. He always wants to be moving. He has auditory processing issues. He's a visual learner. He gets speech twice a week. He gets tutored twice a week. He's getting in-home developmental therapy, since we opted to not put him in the preschool program. And we do our regular life stuff, in addition to our nutrition therapy. They are all pieces of the puzzle.

---

8   DIR/Floortime: Developmental, Individual-differences, Relationship-based model, by Dr Stanley Greenspan
9   ABA: Applied Behavioral Analysis

He is so much more engaged now. His eye contact has improved. He pays more attention to his younger brother. He listens. His receptive language continues to just skyrocket. He'll respond appropriately to familiar directions.

Stephen tunes in and out. He does what he can. Every day is not a great day, but every day is not a terrible day either. Now I look at Stephen and I'm more at peace with his autism. It's been two years since he got diagnosed, and we do what we can from day to day. As long as he's happy, it's good. I do worry about somebody taking advantage of him since he can't talk. Also, I worry about who would take care of him if anything happened to us. My husband and I know what he needs. I don't want him to struggle. That is my biggest worry in life.

What are your hopes for Stephen?

MOM: Yes. My long-term goal is for Stephen to not require twenty-four hour care. I want him to be able to function on his own. He doesn't have to be the star athlete or the straight A student. I just want him to be able to take care of himself. There's this main road that we're paving, and then all these side roads keep opening up. We've met people who are doing wonderful things for kids with autism. There are people out there who want to make a difference and want to understand the disorder. We've met a lot of other parents of kids with autism, and they are amazing people.

God gave us Stephen for a reason. God gave them their children for a reason. We're all working together to try and find out what's the best thing we can do for these children. There's this big puzzle and we're putting in the pieces, one at a time.

— MASON —

4 YEARS | 9 MONTHS

Mason is like any other kid. He just does things a little differently ...
He's a normal kid in many ways and he likes to do normal things ...
It's just a little harder for him to do some things.

Mason's mom

– MASON –

How would you describe Mason?

MOM: It's hard to describe Mason because everything revolves so much around autism with him. You never get time to sit down and think, "Who is he really?" For the most part, he's a fun, loving, mellow and easy going little person, unless you ruffle his feathers a little bit. He likes to have fun. He loves everybody and is always giving hugs. He's very loving to me.

We signed him up for T-ball last year, when he was four. That's when we finally realized that he might not be able to do everything we had expected. We had to deal with the fact that he might not be able to do sports. When he was two to three years old nobody could really tell because all my friend's kids of the same age were developing language and other skills. He didn't really stand out then. In a way T-ball was the first time that we felt like he has autism.

Meanwhile, we're seeing all of the things he's learning. Our friends' kids had done all this stuff a long time ago. They get to take those things for granted. With Mason every little thing he does is like, "Wow! You're so cool. That's so awesome." T-ball for us was a big deal. Anytime he would hit the ball we'd be the loudest people in the stands. It was hilarious.

He's made so much progress. Every little thing is amazing. He went from not saying anything to saying words, like "mom" and "dad." His first sentence was "I love you." We were just amazed. It was huge for him to go to the first day of kindergarten without having a total meltdown. He looked at me with an expression like, "Bye. You can leave me at the gate." I thought, "OK. I guess you don't need me anymore." For him to learn how to put on his shoes now is so awesome. To me those were all huge steps. Every day, it's something. He surprises me when he finally learns the routine of something. If I say, "Go get dressed," and I come in the room and he's dressed, it's awesome.

There has also been huge improvement with his sensory issues. He used to be a lot more bothered by things. Certain kinds of touch would especially bother him. And sounds were a big issue, especially at the mall, or a movie theatre. It was sensory overload. Now, it's better and he seems to be adapting well.

What is he still learning or developing?

MOM: The thing that we're still struggling with is his social skills. Since he's started kindergarten, we've noticed a big growth in him trying to interact with his peers. He's showing more of an interest, but it's still a challenge. He used to have no interest and it was fine if he was just by himself. Now every day he's getting more interested in other kids and activities.

Not knowing if he would be able to develop relationships with people was the most heartbreaking thing for me. I know that academics are important. But for me, my life is very social. It was hard for me to think that in his whole life he might not ever have any friends. So far he's great with his immediate family, cousins, grandma and grandpa, and all. Getting him to go outside of that circle has been a bit challenging. Socialization with other kids is something we're still working on.

His language is coming out more and more. He still has a hard time with his peers because they don't always understand what he's saying and he doesn't always know how to talk to them. But he's trying to say more now. It seems like it's in his head, but it's hard for him to get it out. He'll say something and then look at you with this expression in his eyes, like, "Did you understand?" Now he understands that the words communicate something. He used to point or yell or pull you to what he wanted. Now he's trying to say what he wants. He'll try to interact with his cousins by mimicking them.

He also struggles with basic things in school like writing, and learning his ABCs. He works so hard. He has services Monday through Friday from the time he starts school until two to three hours after school, depending on what day it is. He has behavioral support and occupational therapy at his school. He also has clinic based speech one time per week and clinic based O.T two times a week. We've seen a tremendous improvement in ways that we didn't know if we would ever see.

His little sister is almost two and he's almost five. When we first brought her home, he acted like, "What is this thing coming into the house?" Once she started moving around and getting into his stuff, he wanted her to get away from him. But now they play with each other. They'll chase each other and rough-house together. One of the first times they ever really interacted with each other was when his O.T. let his little sister join in his session. Mason let her sit with him on a swing. They were tickling each other and laughing.

His cousins are his best friends. They are very good with him. Everybody knows Mason's routine. They know how to encourage him and how to talk to him. They're patient with him and protective. Sometimes at the park other kids will say, "Why isn't he talking?" And his cousins will say something like, "He's fine. He just doesn't feel like talking right now." They're always taking him under their wing. It's really great to see.

If someone had not met Mason, but had heard that he has autism, what would you want them to know? Some people can make assumptions when they hear the word autism.

MOM: Exactly. I would want them to know that Mason is just like any other kid. He just does things a little differently. You can't look at him and notice anything different about him. You don't see it on his face. He's a normal kid in many ways and he likes to do normal things. He loves to play with his superhero toys and video games, just like other kids. It's just a little harder for him to do some things.

— DAMIEN —

5 YEARS | 2 MONTHS

It's mostly all about following your child's lead. You try to clue in to what your child's interest is at any given moment. It completely revolutionized the way I interact with the kids.

Damien's dad

– DAMIEN –

How would you describe Damien's personality?

DAD: Describing Damien's personality is emotional for me because his personality is something that we lost. He suffered from the regressive form of autism. Some parents notice some aspects of autism from the time the child was born. But Damien, as far as we can tell, was typically developing up through the age of one year. Another parent once said that having regressive autism is worse in some ways, because you get a glimpse of your child's personality and his potential, and then it vanishes right before your eyes. That is what happened to Damien. Between the ages of twelve to fifteen months, he just disappeared. Our greatest success as a family has been working very hard over the past three years to get our boy back and to recapture his personality. Most of him has come back over the past year. We just didn't give up.

MOM: We have a very biomedical angle on things, because Damien led us that way. Before the autism we knew he had severe allergies. He was getting sick and staying sick. We decided to start removing certain foods from his diet. We had to keep removing foods. The more we worked with that, the more he started to feel and behave better.

DAD: We've been working toward recovery ever since day one. We read a lot of stories about families who combined therapies with medical intervention and have gotten their kids back.

MOM: We were accepted into a study at the university, where they gave him twenty hours a week of ABA home therapy for free.

DAD: And almost immediately after we got his diagnosis, we started with OT using Greenspan's DIR/Floortime approach. Getting him started in OT with a DIR expert was a total blessing. The Floortime model teaches you how to play with your child. It's the things that you do at home, having learned it from your weekly therapy session, that helps the child get better.

MOM: Floortime has made him into an amazing dad.

DAD: For some people playing with kids is intuitive. It wasn't for me. I had more of a tendency to want to force my own agenda onto the kids. Our OT taught me a different way. It's mostly all about following your child's lead. You try to clue in to what your child's interest is at any given moment. It completely revolutionized the way I interact with the kids.

— DAMIEN —

If someone heard that your son has autism, but hadn't met him yet, what would you like them to know about Damien?

MOM: What we would like people to know is that Damien is a sweet boy. I think part of it is autism, and part of it is just who Damien is. Most kids at some point learn how to manipulate situations. He never has. He doesn't play mind games. His personality is not complicated. Obviously, there are other things that make him difficult. But, he's a sweet boy.

DAD: Some of the components of his personality are uncommon to autism. Even during the severe stages it wasn't difficult to get him to try something new or go to a new place. He always seemed open to new things.

MOM: There are a lot of things about Damien that make us hopeful. He's so happy when we take him to church. He loves the music. He loves the notes on the page, the people singing, and the person playing the guitar. Music is a unique part of his personality. We always sit in the same place, with Damien sitting near the aisle because if there's some good music he has to dance. He gets up and dances right in the aisle. Everybody knows him. He doesn't have that social filter that even young kids pick up. He's just himself.

DAD: There was something magical about the first time he saw his little sister. We had just had the baby and it was Damien's last day of school. His teacher had made a big deal about it. She had brought him up in front of the class and said, "Damien, I hear you have a new sister," and she talked to him about it.

We picked him up on our way home from the hospital. His whole class came outside and hovered around our new baby. The teachers had to move the kids out of the way to let Damien through. He got up to the front of the crowd, saw her, and there was a look on his face that was different than all the looks I'd ever seen before. You could tell that he knew that this little baby was different than all the other babies in the world. He knew that she was a part of him. After that, he started to behave somewhat differently. As time went by, there was more of a social connectedness in our house. It started to fall into place.

He still has a little trouble getting words out. We have to be patient and give him extra time. But, at some point he will get them out. The social piece is the last to come. He does pretty well with one-on-one. But, in a group setting with a lot of friends, he can get quite anxious.

How is he with other kids?

MOM: Damien recently asked me, "Mommy, who is my best friend?" He's starting to understand the concept of friendship. He's talking about it and he seems to want it. It's so sweet. But it makes me cry because he doesn't have the interaction skills to actually make a friend.

DAD: He still struggles with other things as well. He can get quite anxious if there's a lack of structure or we're off schedule. Spring and Winter breaks throw him off a bit, since we don't always have things laid out at the beginning of the day. He gets confused because no one is telling him what he's supposed to be doing from moment to moment. My wife is the one who figured this out. If we see him getting a little upset, she'll get out a white board and make an agenda for the rest of the day. And then he's fine.

MOM: When you have a child with autism, you can't follow the typical developmental charts. They don't apply. You have to make up your own chart. He's totally back on the chart now. He's back on the map. We hope that given a few more years, he might be in a regular classroom. He's making so much progress right now. Our greatest success as a family is getting our boy back.

— CAMI —

5 YEARS | 3 MONTHS

It takes a lot for kids with special needs to grow up in this world. They automatically have lots of challenges ahead of them... The more public awareness there is, the better it will be for these kids.

Cami's mom

How would you describe Cami's personality?

MOM: Cami is so loveable and loving. That's one thing that I'm so glad she didn't lose. She loves to hug and kiss and she says "I yove you." One of her strengths is her fearlessness. She's very active. She loves swinging, climbing, and hanging from things. And, she's fast. She loves being outdoors. She loves water, going in the swimming pool, playing in the ocean. If it's water, she loves it. She also loves counting, in both English and Spanish. She can count up to twenty.

She loves to play with her little pop beads that she makes into necklaces. I bought them to help her with her fine motor skills. At first she just threw them around. Eventually, she started putting them together. They're very small beads. Now she really likes them. She also likes to throw her little yellow ball. I used to try to play catch with her, but she would just stand there, while the ball bounced off her. Now she tries to catch it. And she can throw it back toward me.

What skills is she still developing?

MOM: Cami struggles with her speech. She's definitely trying a lot more, but she has trouble annunciating a lot of her words. There has been improvement in her speech over this last year. There is less echolalia. And she'll imitate more. If you ask her to say a certain word, she'll try to say it. In the past she wouldn't imitate words.

She still struggles with handwriting. She has trouble with her pencil grip. We still don't know if she's left or right handed. She switches. She's doing better with using a fork. Occupational therapy has been working with her on her writing and fine motor skills.

In the past she wouldn't follow commands and now she's a lot better at it. It's hard to keep her still, but she's a little better about staying with activities. She struggles with compliance, like sitting still during circle time. A lot of the time Cami will now complete her school work. She might complain, or have a little fit, but she'll still complete it. She gets little smiley faces when she completes her work.

She's very picky with eating, especially with new food. If you try to have her eat something new she'll look at it, smell it, and that's it. I tend to feed her what she likes, which is actually a pretty good variety. She was pickier when she was younger. She's better now. Sometimes if I repeatedly introduce something new, she will eventually eat it.

She's great now with sleeping. She was about four and a half before she started sleeping through the night. It used to take forever to get her calmed down. And then when she went to sleep it was hit or miss if she would sleep throughout the night. Now most of the time she'll sleep through the night. She has been improving overall.

I got her school pictures today. They get better and better each year. The first year she looked so unhappy. The next year she looked bothered. And this last year, I think she looks really cute. She doesn't have the smile down yet. But at least she's looking at the camera. The littlest accomplishments, things that are just the normal day-to-day happenings for parents with neuro-typical kids, are like she just graduated from college. I'll cheer and congratulate her. It's such a big deal and feels so good. You really appreciate every little step.

What would you like to share with parents who are new to the diagnosis?

MOM: I think that every parent is devastated when they first get the diagnosis. It feels like it's the end of the world. But it's important for parents who have a new diagnosis to know that it's not the end of the world. There is a light at the end of the tunnel. You need to get early treatment for your child. And you need to get a really good support group for yourself. That was important for me.

Now I have a great support group of moms. They drag me with them to all the events. We had a pamper party last Friday. It was awesome. It was all gluten and casein free lotions and other products. We were talking about the casein and gluten free diets and other things that have to do with autism. It really helps. I think that it's important to get together with moms who know what you're going through. I can't very easily get together with friends who have neuro-typical kids. It's just so hard. Luckily we have a big family. We all get together a lot. Her cousins come over all the time.

I have also found online support groups and forums. There is so much information and help out there. If you want information on anything, whether its issues with your IEP, or diets, or whatever, you can find groups who are talking about it. There are answers out there. The Internet is an amazing tool.

I want people to know that kids with special needs are special, for sure. There are some heartwarming stories about what some of these kids can do and be. It takes a lot for kids with special needs to grow up in this world. They automatically have lots of challenges ahead of them. There are a lot of obstacles that they have to go through in life. They have enough to deal with as it is, without having to worry about other people's reactions to them. As parents, all you think about is how to protect you child and make sure they're happy. It's a tough thing to accomplish, because you can't be by their side all the time. Kids at school can be cruel. You just wish the adults out there would be less judgmental. All of the increased awareness really helps. The more public awareness there is, the better it will be for these kids.

— RYAN —
5 YEARS | 7 MONTHS

He doesn't readily show his emotions, but when he does he's very
genuine about it... Ryan is reserved, but joyful, for the most part.
He's having a good time. He's being a kid.

Ryan's dad

– RYAN –

When were your two boys diagnosed?

MOM: Ryan was diagnosed a year and a couple months ago. Kyle[10] was diagnosed about six months later. Ryan received a dual diagnosis. The first diagnosis for Ryan was Pervasive Developmental Delay, Not Otherwise Specified (PDDNOS) and the second diagnosis, from a second opinion, was Asperger's Syndrome. It's very subjective and whoever does the testing will give their own slant to it. There's no real "yes" or "no." It's just, "Well today he's acting this way, so today he's got this." One practitioner spent four hours with Ryan. The other one just a few minutes. But they were both pretty accurate.

How would you describe Ryan's personality?

DAD: Ryan is a little guarded. He doesn't readily show his emotions, but when he does he's very genuine about it. There's actually a mixture of genuine reactions and emotional reactions that he's learned from some of the characters on shows he's watched. He can act out the exact emotion of the characters. Ryan is reserved, but joyful, for the most part. He's having a good time. He's being a kid.

MOM: He has a very serious side too. He can be highly emotional at times. He gets more overwhelmed with the negative side of the emotional scale, like sadness or seriousness. When he expresses happiness, it's usually a huge reaction. It's either there, or it's not.

DAD: It seems like he internalizes everything. He doesn't really open up for communication. He is at that age where he confuses emotions.

MOM: He memorizes dialogue. He does it as a substitute for spontaneous conversation. He is coming out of it, but it's been a long process. Everyone says that he speaks so well. But he's memorized a lot of what he says. He knows when and where to use sentences that he's memorized. That's typical of Asperger's.

It's hard to get him to talk about anything to do with himself. It's like pulling teeth when we ask him questions about his school day. He isn't comfortable talking about things unless it's something that he's memorized. If you ask him about what letters he learned in school that day, or how many kids are in his class, or what his favorite toy is, he can't tell you.

---

10   Kyle, page 2

— RYAN —

Do you have a current favorite story about Ryan?.

MOM: We've had a lot of proud moments when Ryan does something new and unexpected. It's so cool when that happens.

DAD: Like when we got the first, spontaneous back and forth dialogue from Ryan, where it was a real conversation and he's not just copying something off the TV.

MOM: Ryan is very active. He could be an endurance runner. He can keep up with people on bicycles.

DAD: When Ryan is not outside playing on a toy or swinging, he likes to play basketball. We have a soccer ball that he throws into the hoop out back. Ryan is smart. He can write with beautifully formed letters. He knows his numbers up to ten thousand or so. He has known the progression of numbers, since he was about three.

MOM: The requirement to go into kindergarten was to be able to count to twenty, know his colors, and know his ABC's. He's been doing that since he was two. He's obsessed with numbers and letters of any kind. He likes license plates. That's his new thing.

DAD: He has an activity book and he likes to do the dot-to-dot. He's getting into more school-age activities.

MOM: Thank God for the preschool teacher that recommended that we get Ryan tested. She was also able to tell us how to go about having it done. That's what got us started on this. I also started connecting with other people who were able to give us recommendations. Now I'm involved in tons of parent groups and I network with people constantly. This all started less than a year and a half ago. Ryan was diagnosed just after his fourth birthday. And then you have a major learning curve. You sink or you swim. Now, I'm an Olympic swimmer.

DAD: When Ryan started kindergarten, we talked to the principal. We had a lot of special requests and they actually agreed to those special conditions.

MOM: They don't typically assign teachers until August, but we knew before the end of June who Ryan's teacher was going to be. We went to the school, walked around, and took pictures. We met the principal and the vice principal. We went to his classroom, and the library, and played on the playground. We took pictures of all of it. It was all about prepping and priming.

– RYAN –

DAD: As long as Ryan is prepped, he does pretty well. There aren't as many anxiety issues now. He looks forward to the bus coming down the street. Fortunately, the school district has been pretty easy to work with, accommodating, and helpful in getting us what we needed. We have friends that are in similar situations, but the school district is not helping them. You hear horror stories about what they're going through. You fight, or you give up. The parents that give up are absolutely miserable because they don't know what to do. It's being able to envision the long-term benefit. You have to keep trying.

MOM: There has definitely been a lot of progress. We've been doing speech therapy and occupational therapy. We're doing a playgroup over the summer. Right now we're doing horseback riding. We have Ryan in a special needs soccer program. We have some equipment at home, like a weighted blanket and a weighted vest. He's on a special diet for his food sensitivities. It's a lot of activities and a lot of money. Insurance is not helpful. If we had unlimited financial support, we would've done some more with therapies. So, instead we've learned a little bit about everything and what can be done with all of the different methods and techniques. We run our household on an eclectic mix of theories and treatments. It's important to have consistency in the home. We have teamwork, and we have unity, which is important.

DAD: It does seem like all of these things have happened to us are for a reason, because the amount of people that we've met in the process is beyond coincidence. The truth is, I love my kids and I'm real happy.

— ROWAN —

5 YEARS | 9 MONTHS

Rowan is more social than his two brothers, but his anxiety level
is a lot higher because he's a perfectionist.

Rowan's mom

His social interest has been both a strength for him
and a source of conflict.

Rowan's dad

– ROWAN –

How would you describe your youngest son Rowan?

DAD: Rowan is a little more social than his brothers Ayden and Ethan[11], who are also on the spectrum.

MOM: I think that was his saving grace. He didn't have any language up to about twenty-two or twenty-four months. He wasn't even pointing. He never babbled as a baby, but he did have eye contact. Once he started therapy it all came really fast. I think that it was because he had a desire to please. He had that socialness. I think that was what brought him around. He became interactive and learned what he could get from it. Rowan is more social than his two brothers, but his anxiety level is a lot higher because he's a perfectionist.

DAD: Rowan's social interest has been both a strength for him and a source of conflict. If he hadn't been socially interested he likely would have stayed very isolated and never learned language. He is very aware of what is going on around him. On the other hand, Rowan also has an angry side to him. However, it has gotten better. He was about two and a half when we first started him in the zero to three school. He had a hard time being around children other than his brothers. The first day he found the very biggest kid in the school, ran at him, tackled him, and took him down. He was very angry about having the other kids around him. He wasn't comfortable with it.

MOM: Last year in preschool he was in a typical class, around typical peers, which was good because he doesn't have that opportunity at home, since both his brothers are also on the spectrum. He did really well. However, he was in a class of eight or nine kids. He does really well with kids on a one on one basis, but in any group he finds the bully and it is usually the biggest kid in the class. And if there isn't a bully, he antagonizes someone until he turns them into a bully. This year he's in a class of twenty-two and he is having a lot of problems. He thinks that there are a lot of bullies.

DAD: Plus since he is now in grade school, at recess time he has more than just his class to choose from. Rowan and Ethan are practically joined at the hip, so they will play together at recess. Rowan will decide that some of the kids from Ethan's class are the bullies, since they are older. He has gotten into fights with some of them.

---

11   Ayden, page 134, and Ethan, page 108

– ROWAN –

How does he decide that they are the bullies?

MOM: Most of the time it's because they disagree with him, they don't want to play what he wants to play, or they don't follow his rules. The other day his school sent home a picture that he had drawn.

It was three stick figures and they had little spiky mouths and then there was a smaller one and he had a spiky mouth too. I asked him about the picture and he said, "Those are the three recess teachers and the little one is me. The three recess teachers are bullies. They're so mean. They are horrible, mean bullies." He went on and on about how mean they were. And they were just enforcing the rules.

DAD: There was a time when he would fall asleep during the day. When I woke him up he would be convinced that it was morning, because usually when he woke up it was morning. When I said "Rowan, it's time for dinner," he'd say "No, it's breakfast." And if I kept insisting it was dinner time he'd get so angry with me that he couldn't speak to me anymore. He would look up with this tearful look on his face. He'd just walk out of the room and go away because he couldn't talk to me anymore. He thought I was so mean because I was saying it was dinner time and not breakfast time. I was going against his will that it was breakfast. Sometimes I'd not tell him what meal it was and just get him eating.

MOM: Rowan has authority issues. He doesn't see adults as having any authority. We really had to work on who is the boss. It's like he thinks "Is it my turn to be the boss yet?." He also can't handle anything that might appear as negative against him. If the rules are set against something that he wants to be doing, then that's negative against him. He'll put himself into time-out because he gets so angry, and sometimes as punishment to us he puts himself in time-out.

DAD: I think Rowan recognizes that he has a little bit of a short fuse and so he'll take himself out of a situation if it's too much.

MOM: There have been times when he's been a good hour or more in time-out. I would ask him if he wanted to come out of time-out yet and he'd say, "No, I'm not ready. I'm just not ready, Mom." I think it's more of a control issue. He's such a perfectionist. There was a time when he wouldn't draw because he knew that others could draw better than him. Anything that he can't do well right away is not worth doing. We are having a hard time getting him to read because he can't do it right away. It's a struggle.

— ANNABELLA —

5 YEARS | 11 MONTHS

Annabella is very sensitive, emotionally. She loves her brother.
If he cries, she cries. She's also very stubborn. I think that is going
to be her saving grace. She has a real inner drive.

Annabella's mom

What would you like to tell me about Annabella?

MOM: It wasn't like I woke up one day and Annabella had changed. She's always had autism. Some people will say that their child lost their language. That didn't happen with Annabella. This is all we know. I think it's kind of fortunate for us that we never saw a "normal" Annabella.

If someone knew that Annabella has autism, but hadn't met her yet, what would you like them to know?

MOM: Most people have preconceived notions about autism. If I had to describe Annabella in a short caption, I would just say that she's a beautiful little girl all the way through. She's very feminine. She's very lovable. She draws people in. She's mostly happy and content. She likes to smile.

Annabella is very sensitive, emotionally. She loves her brother. If he cries, she cries. She's also very stubborn. I think that is going to be her saving grace. She has a real inner drive. Although she doesn't look at you, she's very observant. She's very keen. She's very visual and can read body language. She understands everything.

She and I have a very close relationship. When I'm upset, she senses it, and she becomes upset. I can get a little tense, with all the scheduling and things. She senses it and she gets tense. I have to watch how I act, because she will feed off of it. She reads me. She knows my tone. She understands.

Annabella can become overwhelmed because of her sensory issues. If you put her in a room and give her too many choices, or if you don't serve her the information in a more structured way, it almost looks like she gets bored or shuts down. She likes to know what's going to happen next.

She won't stay by herself for very long. She will come in the house and seek us out. She doesn't stick with one thing for very long. When she was younger, she would get stuck on things. But as she gets older, she's trying new things and trying to do things in different ways.

What are her talents?

MOM: Annabella has great motor skills. She swims beautifully. Swimming is probably going to be her thing. She likes riding her bike. She's a fast learner. You teach her something one time, and she's got it. She likes playing the piano. She has good auditory perception. She'll go across the keys and listen to the different tones. She likes listening to music. She likes to cut and paste. She doesn't play games. She likes to imitate me. She has watched me cleaning up things. Now when she drops something, she'll clean it up. And, she likes the things she does in occupational therapy. She likes the sensory experiences, like swinging. She likes being upside down.

Initially you have to experiment a bit to figure out what services are best for your child. Over time more information has become available. Eventually you find your way. You're not so overwhelmed. Your daily life becomes a little bit more normal. It doesn't take over your whole life.

What services is she receiving?

MOM: We have a really great team for her. At first, you have to find the kind of therapy you want and what the child needs, and then you go from there. We've finally learned what works best for Annabella, and here we are, three years later. We also checked her out to see if she was a gluten / casein-free candidate. She wasn't. She is allergic to a few things here and there. Otherwise she can eat what she wants.

Dr. Greenspan's DIR/Floor Time approach provided a really good foundation for Annabella. She's been getting DIR/Floor Time since a little before she was two. She has received intensive OT twice a week, speech twice a week, and Floor Time ten hours a week. I am very happy to have had the opportunity to work with Dr. Greenspan. I learned so much from him. I would play with Annabella in his office. He would look at me and say, "Come on, Mom. Have fun. See how she's laughing? Look at that glow in her eyes." He'd say, "Lighten up Mom. Just have fun." I would leave thinking, "Don't look at it as therapy. Just have fun. Get on the floor and have fun." DIR has helped our whole family, because it is about the family.

Many people seem to accept the idea that autistic children can't connect, especially if they can't speak. But, there are little things that they do and things that you can work on to help them come out. It also helps you to understand them better, to sympathize with them, and to put yourself in their shoes.

What is she still learning?

MOM: Annabella is still learning how to talk. She's doing better. She communicates more than she actually speaks words. She communicates physically, and through her different sounds. We know that it is a possibility that she'll never talk. We have to prepare ourselves for that. We're not sure. Her speech therapists feels that there is hope.

I think she's going to be OK. We'll see, one of these days. It's a journey. I feel blessed. It's like when you travel. It opens your eyes and makes you appreciate everything more. Most families with children who have autism just live in their own "country." They don't get a chance to talk to other families or even their neighbors.

There's a lot of ignorance out there about autism. When I talk to people, they often say, "Oh, I thought that once you're autistic, your life is just doomed. That's it." And I tell them, "No. There's hope for these kids. There are different therapies and they can become much more integrated in society. They can emerge. You just need to be consistent with therapies."

— GRIFFIN —
5 YEARS | 11 MONTHS

Griffin is much more complex than he seems on the surface, how he acts, how he's always happy and smiling. The way he sees the world is much more complex. He's got a lot of it figured out.

Griffin's mom

— GRIFFIN —

What would you like to share about Griffin?

DAD: Griffin is a boy who works so hard, because his schedule is so full. On many days, from the moment he wakes up, until the moment he goes to bed, he's working with behavioral therapists, speech, and O.T. He's got such a good attitude. I'm not sure if he really understands why he needs to work so hard. He just does it. And he's doing well.

MOM: One of the meanings of his name, Griffin, is "never say die attitude."

DAD: Language is coming along. His focus is coming along. He's making progress intellectually. He's able to do things and listen and respond.

MOM: When you think he's not listening, he's listening. He has an amazing memory. If he meets somebody, he'll remember their name like six months later. Yesterday he went to get his hair cut. I was going to ask for the same girl, but I couldn't remember her name. He said, "It's Kat." So I went up to her and I said, "What's your name?" and she said, "Kat." He does that all the time.

I was in his Kindergarten class one day and the children were taking turns reciting an apple poem that they had just learned that day. One by one they got up, in front of the class, in front of a microphone and tried to recite the poem. I'm thinking, "Oh no. I don't know if he can do it. I'll have to teach him the poem at home." And meanwhile he keeps saying, "Me, my turn, my turn!" So the teacher says, "Okay Griffin, come on up." I'm thinking "What is he going to say? Are the kids going to laugh at him?" I was sweating bullets. And he goes up front, smiles this big smile, and recites the apple poem perfectly. Only about one out of five of the kids were able to do it, and he was one of them. Afterwards, those that were able to recite the poem received a little apple with the poem written on it. Most of them were so happy with the prize. But he really didn't care about it. He just liked reciting the poem. Of course, I went running up to get the apple so I could put it in his scrapbook to remember the day. He blew me away that he could do that. Even the teacher said that she hadn't known that he was paying attention while they were learning it.

DAD: His brain is wired differently than typical kids. There are a lot of challenges, but there are a lot of positives as well. And with his language coming in he's less frustrated. He can communicate what he wants and needs, as well as what he doesn't want to do. It's really decreased his level of frustration. He can get it out and communicate it and people understand it.

You mentioned that he has a great memory. What are his other strengths?

MOM: Griffin is much more complex than he seems on the surface, how he acts, how he's always happy and smiling. The way he sees the world is much more complex. He's got a lot of it figured out. But he isn't really trying to prove anything.

DAD: He's such a happy boy. I mean it's just little things that make him so happy, whether it's having a bowl of ice cream, or a snack, or jumping on the trampoline. He gets happy about things that a typical boy might not even notice or care about.

MOM: Sometimes when I'm at his kindergarten I'll see the other kids already judging each other. He would never judge anything, anybody. He's like Mr. Peaceful. And despite his situation, he's just really happy.

How is he with other kids?

MOM: With other kids, he always chooses the sweet kids. And he can pick them out of a crowd. And that becomes his favorite person. He can figure out who's the sweetest kid in the class. When kids are mean to him, he hardly notices. He's not really aware. I don't know if it's always going to stay that way, because I hear stories.

DAD: However, being with other kids is probably one of his biggest challenges. He has difficulty knowing how to play, relate, interact, and socialize with other kids. He does a pretty good job interacting with his brother, to some extent. He's good with adults. But interacting with peers is one of his biggest challenges, though his language is coming along.

— GRIFFIN —

MOM: We always thought that his younger brother would be Griffin's protector when he gets older. Then one day, at the park, the roles were reversed. There was a boy who was being really mean to his little brother. Griffin saw it, walked over, looked up at the guy, and smiled. His smile just defused everything. He couldn't even talk yet, but he got in the middle of it and defused the situation. Now, if he notices that someone is sad or crying, he'll say, "Be happy. Be happy." That's all he says. He doesn't really have any more words for what's going on, but he is definitely aware of the situation. Sometimes when I get uptight about him being autistic, I'll look at him and then I'll look at kids who are "typically developing," and I see that he's often much happier. He's a cool guy.

Sometimes, when he has a temper tantrum, I will start worrying, "Oh no. Is this going to get worse or is it going to get better? What am I going to do?" But really, he's only had one temper tantrum in the last six months or so. I tell myself, "Chill out!"

One day I looked at him and thought, "Man, he is working so hard. I am so proud of him." I started focusing on that instead of the difficulties. I had been so depressed and so anxious. I was always worried and wondering "What's he going to do next? What's he going to do next?" And then I realized, "He's freaking great where he is right now!" I think that's when things started getting better around here. It was really hard at first. I was a mess. And he knew it. He can feel it. When we're really excited about what he's done, he gets excited. When you're feeling uptight and stressed, he knows. Like any kid, they know. The key is to just look at him, don't compare. And also don't worry about the future. Just worry about right now.

DAD: That was hard in the beginning, because you are so worried about the future. You have certain expectations and dreams. It all changes. But, at the end of the day it's all about whether or not he's happy, right?

MOM: Yeah, he's doing well. He's doing really well.

— SIX TO SEVEN YEARS —

I'd like people to know that autism is not all that she is. It's just a word. It's just a diagnosis or a label. A label can be pretty static. It describes her in some ways, but it's not all that she is. And she's constantly changing.

– *Josie's mom*

I'm going to brag about her just like I brag about her brother. It's just that the celebrations are going to be over things you wouldn't necessarily celebrate with typical kids. So you celebrate smaller victories.

– *Katie's mom*

You hear that people with autism have a hard time with physical contact, that you shouldn't touch them, and that they need a lot of personal space. I am sure that is true of some people with autism but it's not true with our kids at all. They don't have aversions as much as they have cravings for sensory input. It's different with them.

– *Ethan's dad*

When people ask me, "What is your overall goal for Ryan?" Our goal is to get him to his fullest potential, whatever that potential is. If it's as big as a mountain, we're going to get him there. If it's as small as a hill, we're going to get him there, too. Whatever it is. To get him to his highest potential, to make Ryan the best Ryan he can be, that's our goal.

– *Ryan's mom*

— RYAN —

6 YEARS | 3 MONTHS

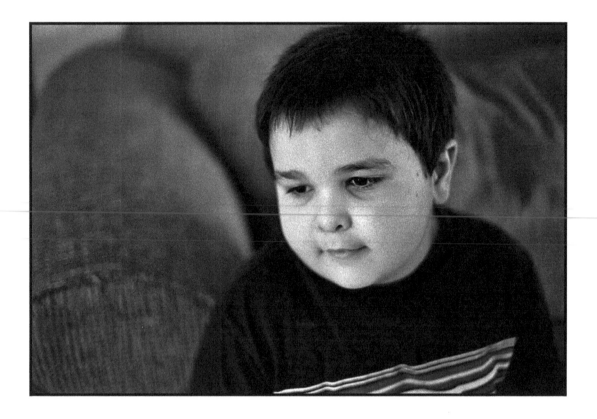

Friends that aren't over to our house that often might say, "I'm so sorry" and "How do you deal with it?" I'll explain that Ryan is a blessing, and he's so joyful. It seems like a lot of their reaction is fear based.

Ryan's dad

– RYAN –

What would you to like people to know about Ryan?

MOM: I have friends that I keep in touch with through email, who haven't met Ryan yet. In describing Ryan, the first thing I say is that he's the sweetest, most loving, most adorable boy, and he is our blessing. We just adore him. He brings this family so much pleasure and so much love. And also, he has special needs. He has autism. He is in special education. He has lots of issues. He's really good with the tangible, but the intangible is more difficult. He can't talk, but he does a great job of communicating. He's always up for doing things and having fun. He enjoys his life.

DAD: Friends that aren't over to our house that often might say, "I'm so sorry" and "How do you deal with it?" I'll explain that Ryan is a blessing, and he's so joyful. It seems like a lot of their reaction is fear based. They just can't imagine it happening to them. The thought is scary. But, you deal with it. You work with it the best way you can. And, most important, you discover how wonderful your child is. That's hard to communicate to others. It's such a personal thing to go through.

MOM: It is fun for us to get a chance to brag about Ryan. We don't often get that opportunity. There's so much information about the problems of autism, and there is definitely a time and a place for that. But I'm glad that we get to also share what is wonderful about our son. I would like the world to know that these kids are beautiful, sweet human beings, and, when they are doing well, you probably won't even notice them. They can look just like any other kid. They are not only about tantrumming in the grocery store. That's a small piece of them, a small symptom of their challenges, which comes out when they get overwhelmed. Sometimes they have trouble going along with what we consider to be normal routine things and they can melt down. But that's not who they are. That's not the essence of these kids, especially Ryan. At his essence he is a sweet-natured, playful, interactive, wanting-to-communicate, little boy.

DAD: It's amazing how happy Ryan is. Every day, the minute he's up, he has the biggest smile. He's giggling. He's running around. He's giving hugs. It's kind of an inspiration because he really values the simple things. He loves being at home and being with the family. He really doesn't have any agenda.

He's this pure, innocent, loving child, and he doesn't push your buttons or do anything to try to irritate you. If he has meltdowns it's because he doesn't understand.

MOM: He's never manipulative. He never tries to bamboozle you. What you see is what you get. And what you see is pure love and pure joy. It's just beautiful. If there's something that makes him happy, he wants to pull you into it. At home he self-regulates very well. He lets us know what he needs. When and how he might overload is a moving mark. So, we listen to him and he listens to us, and we kind of work it out.

DAD: At night, right before he goes to bed, he likes to make a little tent with the couch and pillows. He gets in there and kind of relaxes. It's his little sensory cave. When he's at home, he goes from the swing to the trampoline to the sandbox to his little cave.

MOM: Ryan is an excellent communicator; however, it's not in conventional ways. He talks very little. He has a few tiny words here and there. But he communicates very well. He uses the traditional PECS[12], but he also does more than that. If he wants something, he'll get it and show it to you. He'll point. He communicates through his expressions and how he looks at you. He understands more than he can speak. For instance, if he wants me to take him somewhere, he'll bring me my shoes. I'll tell him, "Oh, Ryan we can't go anywhere right now." But he's not taking "no" for an answer. Next he might bring me my jacket. "No, sorry honey, but we're not going out." Then he'll get my purse, which is funny because my purse is almost as big as he is. He's saying, "Here's your purse, your jacket, your shoes. What's your problem? Let's get going. I've made it so easy for you. Let's get out of here." So, yes, he is very good at communicating what he wants.

Ryan enjoys it when people come over. If he knows that they care about him, he's more interactive. He'll try to communicate. Sometimes it takes a little adjusting on their part because they don't quite speak his language. We tell them, "Just point and say the word. Just point and say fish, or point and say whale, and then he'll make the connection. You're letting him know that you're enjoying this with him."

----

12 PECS: Picture Exchange Communication System

– RYAN –

DAD: Ryan really loves it when we join him in his activities. When you participate in things that he enjoys, whether it's the cave he's built with blankets, or it's playing in the sand with him, or it's copying what he's doing, he really appreciates it. He loves it when you come down to his level. People might say that it's not functional or how can you call that fun. It's fun for us because it's fun for him.

MOM: Ryan's main challenge is that he doesn't get the abstract, and he doesn't understand why the rest of us get the abstract. He doesn't understand the ABCs. To him they are a bunch of meaningless lines. He doesn't understand that the rest of us use them as a tool to read. But, if he wants a cookie, or he wants to play in the water or he wants to go for a drive, he'll figure out a way. Those are the types of thing that he can wrap his thoughts around.

Also, there's so much emphasis on eye contact. But with my son, it can be one or the other. Some kids have trouble processing both listening and giving eye contact at the same time. They have to shut one off to turn on the other one. If I'm demanding that Ryan look me in the eye while I'm talking to him, he might not be listening. So, which one is it? I kind of want him to listen to me. I don't need to be personally satisfied that he's looking me in the eye. I'd rather have him listen to my instructions. If it's one or the other, let's pick listening.

There are definitely things we can learn from him, like his simplicity, his love of life, how he deals with people. He's so warm and welcoming. To be open-minded and not judgmental and be more accepting of people, we can learn all of that from him. We're not trying to pass over his major issues. Yes, he has those. We just want people to be more accepting of his challenges.

People look at him and think, "Oh, poor Ryan." But Ryan doesn't think, "Poor Ryan." Ryan thinks, "Woohoo! It's Monday, and I get to go play, and I get to do what I want to do, and I get to have a good day today." Ryan's not thinking, "Poor Ryan." He is as joyful and loving of his life as anybody on the planet. That's ultimately what I hope people know. He enjoys his life.

When people ask me, "What is your overall goal for Ryan?" Our goal is to get him to his fullest potential, whatever that potential is. If it's as big as a mountain, we're going to get him there. If it's as small as a hill, we're going to get him there, too. Whatever it is. To get him to his highest potential, to make Ryan the best Ryan he can be. That's our goal.

— ROMAN —
6 YEARS | 4 MONTHS

Roman has an amazing sense of spirit. His love gives me strength...
Whenever I'm heartbroken, he knows. He'll wipe away my tears and
give me kisses... He does that for everyone. He is such a love.

Roman's mom

– ROMAN –

What would you like to share about Roman?

MOM: Roman has such an amazing heart. He is very intuitive about people's feelings. He has always been able to sense when people are sad, or when they need love and affection. We've gone through so much heartache with cancer being throughout my family. Roman is always the first person there to lean up against you and love on you. He's my strength and my light. With everything that Roman has gone through, he's so positive. We get so frustrated sometimes, and then he'll say sorry, because he knows that we're all frustrated. Roman has an amazing sense of spirit. His love gives me strength. If I'm crying he'll come to me and say, "Mommy, are you okay?" Whenever I'm heartbroken, he knows. He'll wipe away my tears and give me kisses. That's the best. It's a gift from Roman. He does that for everyone. He is such a love.

Roman has a funny sense of humor. He loves to make jokes and pick on people. He'll tell me, "Uncle Hector is my best friend" and then he'll tell Hector, "Mommy is my best friend." It's a game he plays and then laughs. He plays everybody that way. He'll say, "Ballerina" and I'll say, "You're not a ballerina, you're a football player!" because he loves football. And he'll say, "No. Ballerina." And we'll go back and forth like that. He has so much personality and he's so funny.

In what ways is he still developing?

MOM: Roman is smart academically, but he still struggles in being able to communicate his wants and needs. He has to fight so hard to communicate and he gets very frustrated. He is getting better at regulating himself and calming himself down. Now, every day he's saying more and more. His improvement has been huge, especially since we've started OT using sensory integration. Since starting clinic OT, he's talking and he's potty training. He hasn't had a meltdown in school for two and a half weeks. That's huge since he used to have about five meltdowns a day. We have a sensory diet for him at home and his OT has been working with his sensory issues at school. I've been learning different ways to help him. For instance, if I give him directions both verbally and written he can understand better. If I tell him, "Roman take off your shoes and put them in the closet," he'll just kind of stare at me. But if I write down, "Take off shoes. Put them in the closet," he'll read it and say, "Okay, mom," and he can do it. He can comprehend what he's reading. It's hard for him to attend when I read stories to him. He does better with the read-along books that have audio recordings. He can follow along with the printed words.

And how is he out in the community?

MOM: It used to be hard to go places with him. I never understood, until I started reading about sensory issues. It opened my eyes to the kinds of things he might be processing. Now, when I stop to read his face, I can see that he's being bothered by something or he's really stressed out by something. I'm getting good at seeing that now.

I used to feel locked in my house, because we couldn't go anywhere or do anything. I didn't want to treat him like he was disabled. I didn't want people to be mean to him. At the grocery store people would tell me that I needed to discipline my kid, that I needed to spank my kid, that I needed to do something about my kid. I was so frustrated one time that I said, "Are you a specialist in autism? If you are, then please tell me what to do, because I'm lost." Now I have a sweatshirt that says, "I love my autistic son." I wear that whenever we go out.

I'm the first one now to tell people that my son has autism, especially when we're at a park and there's a bunch of kids. Sometimes I'll go up to another parent and say, "Hi. Is that your daughter over there? My son has autism, and he's probably going to want to play with her, but he doesn't know how to communicate, so sometimes he squeals and makes noises. Is it all right if I go over and talk to your daughter?" Most of the time they're fine with it. Then I'll go over to the child and say, "Hi. Your mommy said I could talk to you. That is my son Roman. He is six years old. He likes to play, but he doesn't know how to talk. He has autism." And often the child will say, "I'll play with him." I'll say, "Okay, thanks." Roman really likes to be social. He'll squeal, and he'll sing songs, or he'll say funny things. Often times the kids will later tell me, "He's cool." It's especially important with older kids. It helps if they understand.

– ROMAN –

As much as he is a wonderful amazing child, it sounds like there are some rough times. What helps you get through those?

MOM: What really helps get me through all of this is prayer, and my family and friends. I get so many emails telling me that people are praying for us. Roman is surrounded by so much love. My ex-husband and I are co-parenting and we're making it work. We do it for Ro. I wouldn't be able to make it if I didn't have my family praying for me, encouraging me, and supporting me. It really helps, because it can be a battle every single day. Getting him dressed in the morning can be a battle because I don't know what side of the bed he's going to wake up on. I don't know if he's going to want to put on his socks and shoes, or if he's going to scream and kick that morning. It's all about unconditional love. I feel that my purpose is to be Roman's mom, and as long as I ask God to give me the strength every single day and do the best that I can as his mom, then everything will work out. I've always wondered if Roman will understand the concept of faith, the concept of love, the concept of God. I know that he loves me, and I know that he has faith that I'll be there.

— PAUL —
6 YEARS | 5 MONTHS

Paul creates things in his mind. He has a bunch of inventions that he's come up with... His imagination is immense. He's already, just for fun, designed a whole video game... It's incredibly detailed.

Paul's mom

– PAUL –

How would you describe Paul?

MOM: Paul is a really loving guy. He's going through something right now because he constantly comes to me and asks for a hug. But, it's only at home. He doesn't want me to show him affection in public.

Paul has Asperger's. He's an extreme guy. He's very stubborn, even when it doesn't make sense to be stubborn. He'll inflict his own punishments. Some tiny thing will happen and he'll say, "I guess I can't watch TV forever." He's very dramatic and hard on himself. He is getting better, but it's still difficult.

Paul is a sensitive boy. He's a perfectionist. He's always had an issue with losing. He couldn't lose a board game. If he wasn't at the top of his class he would see that as losing. He can't accept even the smallest bit of failure. Paul doesn't tantrum anymore. Instead, he pouts or he'll just look grumpy. He won't explain to me what's happening with him. But he recovers more quickly now. In the past if something happened his whole day would be ruined. He's doing much better.

How is Paul's sense of humor?

MOM: Yes, he does have a sense of humor, which is interesting because he doesn't always get if things are funny or not. He understands a joke and thinks it's funny but he likes to create jokes and sometimes they're not funny. Of course, he will think that they're very funny.

Paul has tremendous difficulty making a decision when there are too many choices. He's very creative. Once he makes a decision, with creative writing for instance, he will write a beautiful story. But getting started is very difficult. There's too many thoughts in his head; too many choices. He gets frustrated because he can't start. I think that's part of his brilliant mind. He has so much going on in his head. I think he needs to analyze it and reanalyze it and think about it again.

He's not a planner. It doesn't occur to him that some things take multiple steps. He ends up rushing through projects because he doesn't have a sense of the steps that are needed and the time it will all take. He just goes from the idea to the end product. The in-between is hard for him

– PAUL –

to map out. But he does really well in school, except with creative writing, mostly just because he can't get started. Once he does, he does very well. Also, he thinks about things in such details. He wants to put all the details in his story. He has to figure out how to make all that fit and sometimes he can't get it done in time.

He would like to be a race car driver, as well as an inventor/scientist. Paul creates things in his mind. He has a bunch of inventions that he's come up with. He's drawn them all out. His imagination is immense. He's already, just for fun, designed a whole video game. He's drawn it all out, too. It's incredibly detailed. He maps out all of the contingencies, like if this happens, that's going to happen, and this character will do this or that.

Paul has always had sensory issues. He's sensitive to some kinds of touch. He gets the heebie-jeebies. He gets real squirrely and tries to get away. The other day he actually told me that I hurt him. I just had my hand on his shoulder. He was letting me know that the way I was holding him was bothersome to him.

He has lots of feeding issues, especially with textures. When he was little he didn't like any clothes on him except for shoes on his feet. He always guarded his hands and feet. He would want his shoes back on after his bath at night. He wanted to sleep in his shoes. We also had lots of problems with teeth brushing.

He loves speed. He loves to run and ride his bike or scooter really fast.

Paul has a select few friends. This year Paul wanted to make sure that a certain number of people had his phone number over the summer. He's been asking me, "Can I call so-and-so?" He's seeking friendships, but he still doesn't get it. There are some parts of it that he wants, and then he ends up getting his feelings hurt because he doesn't understand. But he has grown.

Paul is in a gifted classroom and those kids are, by nature, loners. I have volunteered in the classroom. I didn't see him talk to his neighbors. I don't know if it's because he doesn't have a personal connection with those particular kids. One time while I was there they had a class party and he was reading at his desk. They were supposed to be eating and socializing. But I didn't bother him. If he was more comfortable reading, it was O.K. with me. He's real close with the kids that he does talk to. I just think he doesn't share himself with everybody, so many of them don't get a chance to know him. I wish he could be more outgoing because he's an amazing little guy. He's really fun but he's shy, unless you're one-on-one with him and then you can't get him to stop talking.

What does he like to talk about?

MOM: Paul mostly likes to talk about video game strategy. He really plans out his strategy. He can't wait to get back to the game to see if the strategy works to get him on to the next level. He's constantly problem solving in his head. Sometimes he will initiate conversations about other things. Occasionally he'll ask, "So, how was your day today?"

I truly do not see it as a disability. That's why I've rarely used the label. He has issues that are maybe a little bit more severe but everyone has something. Too many people hide behind a label and make it a disability or believe in the label so much that it cripples them. Eventually, you have to get over it or deal with it. I haven't told Paul or his brother[13] that they are on the autism spectrum. They understand that they have food allergies. They understand that they have vitamin deficiencies. They understand that they need speech and OT but they don't know why. I think that it will be special to be able to talk to them when they're older about the struggles when they were younger and how far they've come. I wholeheartedly believe that they're both going to be just fine.

---

13   Paul's brother, Alexander, page 130

— KATIE —

6 YEARS | 8 MONTHS

The more worth we place on her words, the more progress we've
made. Otherwise, she still doesn't understand why we live on
"Planet Words," or why we need words at all because it's so clear to
her that life is fine without them.

Katie's mom

How would you describe Katie?

MOM: Katie is fun. She's a happy kid. She truly is all love. Katie's a little hard to get to know, but if she loves you, it's pure love. There's no angle to it. Once people get to know her, they're totally captivated by her. I was telling my husband, "It's pretty great being Katie." She has simple wants. I don't think she's ever going to care where her clothes come from. She's never going to be the nails and spa treatments type girl. Maybe she would not have been that way anyway, but that's definitely not who she is now. She really keys in on what's important: are you fed, are you clothed, are you not being annoyed? If so, then she's happy and good to go. She figured out at a very young age that if nothing is tormenting you then you better hold on and be happy. It took me thirty years to figure that out. She has this attitude about life that we can learn a lot from. It's like she's an old soul. She's kind of boiled life down to what is important. That's how she lives her life.

The irony is that the only day of the year that I'm really bummed is Mother's Day. For whatever reason, Mother's Day is the day. You think about what it could have been. There are tough times. It's little moments that'll get to me and I'll be sad. Mother's Day is the day that really wears thin. Otherwise, maybe on three days out of thirty, a part of the day will be rough. But in the last six months, now that she has more complicated words, it's been so much easier.

Because she's not typical, every time she gets a bruise we'll get asked how she got it. When she was in first grade I was actually asked how she lost her two front teeth. How many parents of first graders get asked, suspiciously, about how the child lost their two front teeth? Since she can't talk, everyone is more on alert. The more worth we place on her words, the more progress we've made. Otherwise, she still doesn't understand why we live on "Planet Words," or why we need words at all because it's so clear to her that life is fine without them.

Katie is in a general education setting, with an aide. Just this last month, her aide started a buddy program. The classroom has the daily line leader and a few other daily special tasks. Now being Katie's buddy is one of the special daily things. The kids just love it. It's become cooler than being the line leader. They all want to be Katie's buddy. Katie loves it. The kids are so accepting.

– KATIE –

How is she with other kids?

MOM: Katie is starting to seek out and recognize social situations. She has great taste. She picks kids you would want your child to play with. Obviously it's a self-selection, because it's also a special kid who would be willing to play with her. I understand that. The two girls I'm thinking of are just kinder than kind, and patient. These are who you'd want your child to choose as friends.

We don't have to deal with some things that parents are going to deal with or worry about. I'm never worried about her choosing a friend who is a bad influence, because the bad influence child is never going to choose her. And she's not going to choose them.

For her birthday last year we took her to Goofy's kitchen at Disneyland. The first talking character was Alice, and Alice figured out that they had a very special guest dining with them. After that all the characters fawned over Katie. She was so excited that she almost cried. She had never been able to have her picture taken with a character because she had never had enough patience to stand in line.

Now once a month a local theatre has movie screenings that allow kids to be kids. She loves it. The kids can walk around and make noises. Katie can walk up to the screen, or do whatever she wants. And the typically developing siblings don't really care, which was a great thing. Her brother got to go to the movie theater with the whole family and watch a movie. It wasn't about tolerant adults. It was about tolerant kids. They didn't even notice the behavior that was going on around them. It was like white noise that they didn't even catch. The lights are kept on during movie. The sound was lower, so it wasn't blasting. The kids could get up and move around. It was wonderful.

How is her relationship with her brother?

MOM: Her brother is very proud of her and her accomplishments. The fact that she wants to be around him really helps. I came into work about two years ago, excited that Katie and her brother had got in a fight. People said, "We're sorry." And I said, "No. It's the greatest thing. That means that they want to be together. It's means that they know that each other exists." They had never fought, because Katie had no interest in him. But all of a sudden she was interested in him. They started fighting, and it was just music to me. Of course you want them to move forward and not fight. But that first time was good because it was a deeper connection between them. He's in her "club" now. She really likes him. And he's so good with her. He's a much better person than he would have been without her.

I'm going to brag about her just like I brag about her brother. It's just that the celebrations are going to be over things you wouldn't necessarily celebrate with typical kids. The other day she was at school and I asked, "Where's your sweater?" She said, "On the couch." I was floored. That was the first time she'd ever answered a question other than "yes" or "no." So I wanted to give her a high five, but on the other hand she was supposed to have brought her sweater with her, so it was this mixed thing. Of course, I told everyone at work that she said, "On the couch." Everyone at work thought that she should get an ice cream for saying that. So you celebrate smaller victories.

— LANCE —

6 YEARS | 8 MONTHS

Lance really likes to have fun. That's one of his best characteristics. He's all in it for a good time... Honestly, I don't care about the diagnosis. There's no cure, but I would like him to be in recovery. He has great potential.

Lance's mom

– LANCE –

What would you like to share about your son?

MOM: Lance is happy most of the time. He will go through a little bit of sadness every so often, where he kind of cries for no reason. I haven't seen that in a while, though. He's very sensitive. When his little sister cries, he cries. But, for the most part he's very happy. He has a sense of humor. Sometimes he'll say something, and then say, "That's funny, huh?" and I'll say, "Yeah that is funny."

Lance really likes to have fun. That's one of his best characteristics. He's all in it for a good time. And he's super smart. He's six and he can read. Actually, he's been reading since he was three. He really enjoys it. He loves to read and he understands what he's reading. I think that's one of his great qualities. He has a great imagination, which I never had to teach him. That was already part of the puzzle of who he is. He has great play skills. It's amazing. He loves to do dress up and he loves to act out things. It's great. It's so much fun.

Last year he did T-Ball. It was a lot of effort in the beginning for him to learn how to stay focused and learn the rules. But by the end he was just like all the other kids. They were pitching. He was hitting. He was running the bases. And this was a team of typical kids. It was beautiful. It was the best experience we've had with him. It was his first experience in an organized sport. He was five. It was so cool. We would take our behaviorist with us, and they would help us with the behaviors. It was just amazing to have him be part of a team. Everyone was so nice. No one made fun of him. And by the end he was just like everyone else. It was great.

He's really trying to learn to use a skateboard or a scooter. He tries really hard, but it is difficult for him because it takes a lot of attention, concentration, and focus. He also needs to have better bilateral coordination and balance. But he's trying. He can ride a tricycle, and he can ride a bike with training wheels. He's really good with those. And those things are really important to me. Lance really needs the physical exercise. He does really well with physical activities.

Are there things that he still struggles with?

MOM: Lance struggles with change. In school, he has difficulty changing from a preferred activity. When we go to Disneyland, he wants to only go on his favorite rides. Also, he struggles with attention and focus. That really brings down his potential. He enjoys his verbal and hand stims. But that's something I think he uses to decrease his anxiety.

He's very sensitive to his sister's cry. He wants to know if she's okay. He wants to know what she needs so she'll stop crying. I think he gets it that she's not leaving, that she's here to stay and that she's his sister. He had to draw a family picture the other day at school and he automatically included her. I thought that was great. He drew a little miniaturized picture of her. When they asked, "Who's that?" he said it was his little sister. That was great.

He struggles with his speech, especially with clearly expressing his feelings. When I pick him up from school, I'll ask him how school was that day. He'll tell me, "Oh, school was fine." I'll ask him what he did that day. I can see that he's really trying to tell me, but he has a hard time. The ideas are up there, but he doesn't exactly have the language. He has trouble making it come out in a way that I would understand. It's hard for him to put all those words into a sentence that I would get. One day I when I asked him what he did that day in school, he said, "Balloons flying up in the air." Later, when I asked at school what they had done that day, they told me that at recess he had played a balloon game with some friends. The balloon would be thrown in the air and they would chase it.

How is he with friends?

MOM: He will play physical games with his friends. And he will say a few words. But he's not very confident and you can see it in his face. He's not confident about his speech and he's very shy and he's very nervous, because of his language. I think he knows that not everyone understands him. It takes him a long time to get comfortable with someone before he opens up and starts talking. He's afraid that they're not going to understand him, and he's going to get frustrated.

– LANCE –

He's not always able to tell me why something bothers him. It's really difficult for him. My biggest fear is that something would happen to him and he wouldn't be able to tell me. He wouldn't be able to tell me if someone had picked on him at school. He has told me, "I'm scared, I'm afraid," but he's not able to express why he is scared or what made him afraid. He doesn't like haircuts. He'll say, "I'm afraid. It's scary." When I ask him why, he'll say, "It hurts," and point to his ears. It hurts his ears. That's a big thing for him to be able to tell me why something bothers him.

Lance does work really hard. I tell him that he's the hardest working kid I know. He goes to school a half hour early to get the sensory piece in. He's at school all day. He has OT or speech most days after school. On top of that he comes home and gets ABA every day. Lance gets ten hours/week of ABA with an agency that addresses his behaviors from all angles, including recognizing his sensory needs.

Honestly, I don't care about the diagnosis. I never have. I don't care about the word autism. There's no cure, but I would like him to be in recovery. I would like him to be on his way to having no signs and be the best that he can be. He has great potential. I've always believed in him.

— MAX —

6 YEARS | 11 MONTHS

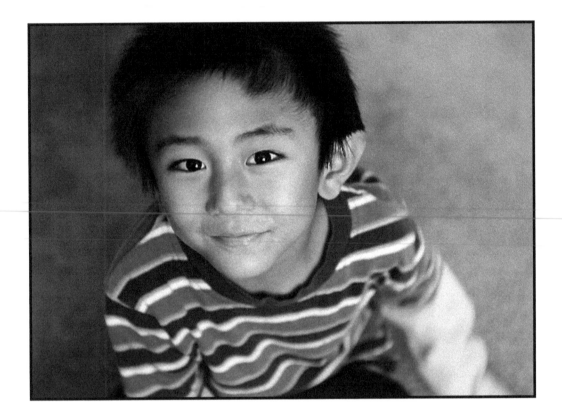

Max knows who is genuine and who is faking it. He's so good at reading people that it can be scary sometimes ... He might lack some social skills but something about him attracts people to him ... It's so mysterious.

Max's mom

What would you like to share about Max?

MOM: Max didn't get a diagnosis of autism until he was five. We didn't hear Max talk until he was four or five. We didn't even know how his voice would sound. Now every time we talk with him it's like a song. We could just listen to him all day long. His voice is so cute.

DAD: A lot of people are surprised that he can talk so well now.

MOM: Max used to cry all the time. For the longest time we couldn't figure out if "crying Max" was the actual Max. We thought that he would be like that for the rest of his life. We thought that he was going to be angry and sad all the time. He would cry for five hours straight. No matter what we did he would not stop crying. We would try feeding him. We would try changing him. We would try everything to make him comfortable. But nothing worked. We didn't know what was wrong. Eventually, we didn't have any more ideas, so we just stopped trying. From the time he was born he cried a lot. We thought that our parenting was to blame and that there was something definitely wrong. We just could not figure out this boy.

It seems like Max is aware of what had been going on when he was little. One time we were at the dining table, just casually talking, and he said, "Mommy." I said. "Yeah." And he said, "When I was baby, I cried a lot." I thought he was talking about babies in general. I said, "Yeah, babies do cry a lot." Then he said, "No, I cried a lot." So I asked, "Do you remember why you cried so much?" He said, "Because I was missing you mommy." I thought, "Wow, that's so profound."

Another time he said, out of the blue, "I feel happy. I feel like Me." I thought, "No. He didn't just say that." It was like something out of a movie. That's when I felt like, okay, maybe we are doing something good here. Some parents feel guilty about dragging their kid to occupational therapy, speech therapy, and whatever. We do sometimes feel that way. We worry that maybe the child isn't ready to do all this and that maybe we're just pushing them too much. But now we don't feel that at all. We know that it was all worth it.

– MAX –

Max is really good at getting smiles from other people. He just really knows people. I think kids with disabilities have souls that are just so pure that when they look at other people they know right away if that person is good or bad. They can sense their intentions. They seem to see right through people. Max knows who is genuine and who is faking it. He's so good at reading people that it can be scary sometimes.

It's hard to describe it in words. When you're with a person like Max, it's like your whole soul is cleansed or something. You don't have to pretend. You can just be yourself and they will totally accept you. He might lack some social skills but something about him attracts people to him. People are drawn to him. It's so mysterious.

DAD: Even people working in busy places like the metro stations or the airport listen to Max when he talks to them. We try to move him along because they look too busy, but he just talks in his own pace.

MOM: And people want to listen to him. He pulls them in.

DAD: He has charm. Our older son as well, but Max has a special something

How are his social skills with other kids?

MOM: His social skills are so good now it's scary. He wasn't like this until this year. He also had self-injurious behavior. He used to bang his head against the wall or the floor. Now as his aggressive behaviors have decreased, his social skills have increased. Before, we had to prompt him to interact with other kids. Now he is the one that wants to share everything. He has a group of kids who want to hang out with him. It seems like everything he does is so fascinating to the other kids. He still doesn't know how to stay on topic. Also, he might start a conversation in the middle instead of starting with, "Hi Shay my name is Max." But those are higher level skills.

How has Max influenced your life?

MOM: With my kids, especially Max, I never realized that I could feel so much joy over little things. I'm very competitive when it comes to academics. I always want to be first and I strive for the best. I never thought that there were people that, no matter how much they tried, they just couldn't do it, unless it was modified or done in different ways. So for a person like me to have kids like my kids was definitely eye opening. My attitude towards people with disabilities has definitely changed. I used to just feel sorry and sad and almost pity them. But now it's not as big a deal to us. It's still a lot of hassle every day. We do things that normal families don't have to do. But it's become part of our life. And because Max is improving, my older son feels much more secure. He told me this morning that in the past when Max had a bad day he would feel bad too. He always feels like he has to protect Max. I told him that is nice that he feels that way, but I made sure that he understood that it's our responsibility as parents to protect them and not his responsibility.

As parents, we accept our son. It's funny that other people are so dismissive and tell us not to worry, he'll be okay. We've already accepted him so why are we having this conversation about whether you want to accept him or not. It's interesting how other people react to Max's diagnosis. People seem to think that they need to react. The best thing people can do is just to listen to what we have to say. They don't have to figure out things. All they have to do is just listen.

— GOVERNOR JEFF —

7 YEARS | 1 MONTH

Governor Jeff is not that hard. Actually, a lot of the time, he acts better than some typical kids That's the other side of it. When he first went to the special education class, I was surprised at how great the kids in his class were. But I don't want to sugar coat it. We still have challenges.
Governor Jeff's mom

– GOVERNOR JEFF –

What would you like people to know about your son?

MOM: Governor Jeff is a great child. I've learned so much from him. I would describe his personality as sweet and active. I think one of his best skills is his memory. And he loves music. He has a really beautiful smile and he's a pretty happy kid. I love him and accept him. I don't get mad when he does the things he does, like banging on things, or making noises. For him, he's talking. My close friends know him and accept him. They don't tell him to stop making noises. They know that he has to have his outlet. He likes hugging. He likes the pressure. He likes to ride his big wheel or his scooter. These kinds of things help to calm him. He likes walking in the mall. We do a lot of walking.

Governor Jeff has some words that he uses. And he has a little text-speak board that he's learning how to use. Otherwise, he'll take my hand to show me something, and I have to figure it out. I've gotten pretty good at figuring out what he wants. Thank goodness that he points now.

This year he started being more sociable. He used to not really care. He'd just do his own thing on the playground. He'd climb. He'd go down the slide. He'd bang on things. Now, he tries to get kids' attention. He's more interactive and he wants to play. Before, he didn't really want to be bothered. He was just having a good time with himself on his own. But now, he really wants to play.

He was such a picky eater. He's better now. That had been a major stressor for me, the whole food thing. Then I just had to let go. As long as he's healthy and he's eating it was O.K. It's getting better. We're working on it little by little.

Sleeping had been a major issue with Governor Jeff, since he was born. He didn't want to go to sleep. He'd be up every two hours or so. That was really hard. Now he sleeps almost every night. Maybe twice a month, he might have a night where I'm up, and I'm not going to get any sleep. I try to have a good attitude about it, because I just have to do what I have to do. He's doing much better.

How old was he when he got diagnosed?

MOM: He was two and a half when we first got the diagnosis and I was obviously devastated, like any parent would be. I was messed up. If I didn't believe in God as my son's main source of help, I would still be messed up. I'm not discounting all his therapies, because I believe in them. We did the recommended therapies, OT, speech, ABA, but a big part of it is my spiritual beliefs. I'm very strong in what I believe. I see beyond autism.

Nobody wants their child to have to go through this challenge. But, I don't believe that God would do anything evil. Of course, I wasn't happy. As the parent, you blame yourself. My husband has been my rock. He's really strong. When Governor Jeff was diagnosed, my husband just said, "Okay." Some people fall apart. But he was strong. He saw Governor Jeff overcoming it from day one. It was beautiful. It helped me.

Governor Jeff is not that hard. Actually, a lot of the time, he acts better than some typical kids. That's the other side of it. These kids can be great. I didn't know that when he was diagnosed. When he first went to the special education class, I was surprised at how great the kids in his class were. But I don't want to sugar coat it. We still have challenges. Governor Jeff still wants to bang everything. He pushes on his chin with his hand to get extra pressure. He claps. He does those kinds of things.

How is he when you go out into the community?

MOM: He's pretty good, now, when I take him out in public. But at first it would be challenging. When we'd take him to a restaurant, he'd cry and want to leave. Nobody in a restaurant ever said anything, but you could tell people were looking. You're human, and you can get your emotions hurt. But I'm tougher now. When you first get the diagnosis you're soft. Now it's like, "Okay. Whatever. We're here." If someone came up to me and said something I'm ready for it now. It hasn't happened yet, but it will.

– GOVERNOR JEFF –

Governor Jeff might do some things that are different, but as far as personality, he's just like any kid. He's just Governor Jeff. I don't like him to be classified only as an autistic kid. I'm not denying it, but I'd like him to be known as Governor Jeff. I see him beyond autism. I don't like him categorized. He's not just a list of traits. He's just a kid like any other kid.

Everybody has challenges. If it's not their kids, it's something else. Maybe it's someone in their family. It's just life. So, it's not going to do any good to get mad. You might as well enjoy it and grow from it. That's what I'm doing through Governor Jeff. I'm not giving up.

When you have a child that has any challenge, autism or whatever, you can become a better person. You have the opportunity to develop compassion and to grow. You're more understanding and caring of typical kids and of kids with challenges. You have to allow yourself to change. I know people can get really depressed. I want them to know that it's not that bad.

I'm not saying that I don't get negative, and that there are times when I have to be firm with him. But my focus is on the positive. I try to be positive with everything and everyone. People worry too much. It's all about staying positive. I think people have to have vision. You have to make the circumstances that you want. And that's how I feel about Governor Jeff.

— JIMMY GEORGE —

7 YEARS | 2 MONTHS

You worry when you have a kid with autism that kids are going to be mean, they're going to call him names, and they're going to treat him differently. But, no. The kids in his first grade class are even nicer to him. They love him, because he's so sweet and easy. They try to help him.

Jimmy George's mom

– JIMMY GEORGE –

How would you describe Jimmy George?

MOM: To me Jimmy George has the happiest soul, with a deep heart and a very kind spirit. I don't think he's ever shown aggression towards anyone. He has this natural way of bonding with people. He's very approachable. He's a gentle loving person and he makes me smile. It's like he has this instinct about him, especially since his father passed away. As we're coming into the house and I'm holding groceries, he'll hold the door open for me. I didn't teach him to do that. I think he has this natural ability to read people, to sort of feel them. And he knows when you're hurting. Sometimes I think autism is a strength. At least it is for him. He has something that other people don't, like an extra sense.

When we first found out that Jimmy George had autism, I looked at my husband and said, "What are we going to do." And he said, "Nothing. We'll just take care of it." And that was it. You know, what are you going to do? You just take care of it. Jimmy George was still Jimmy George. He was almost three when we found out. I feel like Jimmy George thinks of it as, "Mom, I got to do this because I got to do it."

Having Jimmy George changed my life. I think that when I had him I became an adult. He gave me a purpose. I felt, "This is what I want to do. I want to take care of Jimmy George." When I was younger, I remember thinking that I didn't want to have kids. And then all of a sudden I went from having one kid to wanting to have ten. I'm happy that I have Jimmy George.

Before Jimmy George was born, my husband and I owned a business. After he was born I gave up working to be a full time mom. Even before the diagnosis, I was going to be a stay at home mom. Before his birth I always had a job. I always had something to do. What I'm doing now is very different. And I love it. I work as a one-on-one aide at a wonderful local preschool program for children with special needs. It's all about love with these kids. All day long there's just love. When I started working there I thought, "This is what I should have been doing all along." Maybe I don't have any other kids of my own because I have all these kids at school. That's the best reward ever. And I'm learning more about how to deal with Jimmy George's disability. I'm more involved with what's going on with him, because I can learn through the other kids. So it's the perfect place for me.

How is he in the classroom and with the other kids at school?

MOM: Jimmy George has been great at school. He's in a typical first grade. He has a one-on-one aide and he gets pulled out for services. He pretty much can do the work that the other kids do. He's above his age for reading. He has more books than toys. You worry when you have a kid with autism that kids are going to be mean, they're going to call him names, and they're going to treat him differently. But, no. The kids in his first grade class are even nicer to him. They love him, because he's so sweet and easy. They try to help him.

What skills is he still developing?

MOM: He still is developing his verbal skills. He doesn't use his words all the time. He won't tell me when he's in pain or why. He doesn't engage in social interaction with his own peers. He interacts more with adults, because adults are more predictable than children. When his peers want to hug him, he's starting to hug back, because he knows that they're not trying to hurt him. He's processing all that and it's starting to sink in. Today I saw a little girl in his class hug him and when he hugged her back I almost cried. Sometimes my nephew wants to play with Jimmy George. Jimmy George used to back off. Now they know each other better and they can wrestle. That kind of physical play with his peers is coming along.

Sometimes I'll take him to a toy store and tell him he can pick out a toy. I'll ask, "Do you want this one?" After he plays with it for a few minutes, he'll give it back. I can never buy him a toy because he never picks anything. He doesn't have a preference. Most kids bother their parents asking for toys, asking them to buy this and that. I pray for the day that my son bugs me to buy him a toy. It's true. That's one thing about him. But he gets a lot of toys anyway.

He does struggle with some things. It took me six years to potty train him, because it didn't seem to have any meaning for him. That was the hardest thing, having a child in kindergarten still in diapers. Also, his eating habits are really bad and he has some sensory sensitivities. But he's great with sleeping. He might be a bit hyper, running up and down the stairs. But when I ask Jimmy George to take a shower or something, I don't have to bug him to do it, he just does it on his own.

When I tell him it's time to go to bed, there'll be no whining. He gets right into bed and under the covers. He'll say "I want music." I put on classical music and he'll listen to it until he falls asleep.

He will use scripting, but he can step out of it. He uses it appropriately most of the time, although not always. Sometimes he'll use it to tell me something. He also likes to get me involved in his scripting. He's very entertaining. He usually doesn't get stuck, repeating them over and over. If he does seem to be stuck I just enter into the scripting with him and then change it slightly so it becomes a conversation between the two of us.

Once, when I had just finished doing something, and he said, "You go girl," which he had picked up from a children's book. Another time he had popcorn while he was watching TV. I walked in and saw that he had spilled popcorn all over the carpet. I was about to scold him for making a mess, when he looked at me and said "Free popcorn for everyone!" I was laughing so hard, I had to leave the room. He had used his words appropriately. How could I scold him? I just made him help me clean it up. He's such a character.

About two years ago, we were at church and to keep him quiet I had given him a lollipop. The priest was reading scripture and said, "There will be one kingdom, one shepherd," and Jimmy George yelled out "One lollipop." "Well," I thought, "At least he's paying attention." But that was the last time I gave him a lollipop during mass and now we sit in the crying room.

How has Jimmy George influenced your life?

MOM: I'm glad that no one ever told me or predicted it, because I would have panicked. Now that I have this life I'm so thankful. It all happened so gradually. It was a nice transition. I wouldn't take it back. It never gets old with Jimmy George. If I didn't have him, I wouldn't be here. Not only did he give me a reason to keep going after my husband died, but he is so easy to be with. He helps me. It's like he watches over me. It's that extra sense he has. I always feel safe with him. Jimmie George has such great characteristics. You look in his eyes and you can see a lot. He has a purpose. His spirit is amazing. It really is.

— AMBRYN —
7 YEARS | 4 MONTHS

As Ambryn is getting older, she's allowing people more into her world. For many years we could only witness it from the outside... She's opening up and sharing more, talking more. There has been a huge change in the last six months or so. That's been really cool.

Ambryn's mom

How would you describe Ambryn?

MOM: Ambryn is very unique. She has always had great language. It seemed like what she lacked in gross motor skills she made up with in speech. Her vocabulary is pretty extensive and she's very detailed in her descriptions. She is still very black and white. If you say, "It's raining cats and dogs," she'll take it literally. At school they're working on her cognitive reasoning. She also struggles with math word problems. She does really well with spelling, because she has really good memory. But she has a hard time with reasoning and abstract thinking.

DAD: She's also a very good artist. She draws constantly. She'll cram all this stuff onto one piece of paper, like puppies and sharks and all kinds of things. It's so cool.

MOM: As Ambryn is getting older, she's allowing people more into her world. For many years we could only witness it from the outside. She's also more a part of our world now. She's opening up and sharing more, talking more. There has been a huge change in the last six months or so. That's been really cool.

DAD: And she's asking questions, which is something she never used to do. She also has a wonderful sense of humor.

MOM: She has started to laugh at things and make jokes.

DAD: She used to just watch a TV show because she liked to watch. But now she gets the humor and laughs appropriately when things are funny.

MOM: Ambryn never use to play. She didn't know how. Her older sister taught her. It's only in maybe the past year that Ambryn plays and it's really because of her sister.

DAD: Her sister is a very good teacher. Her older brother used to be Ambryn's wrestling buddy. She still likes to beat on him.

MOM: Her older brother and sister have been so supportive, not only of her but of me and of how much time needs to be spent one-on-one and devoted to Ambryn. It's got to have been hard on them, especially when she was younger.

You mentioned other people's reactions when Ambryn is having a difficult day.

MOM: Other people's perception can be hard. Unfortunately when you see a child misbehaving or having a tantrum you just automatically assume that the parent needs to do a better job of handling the child. There is a button that says "Don't judge. My child has autism." It would be better if we didn't need to have a button like that. It would be better if people were more educated about the disorder. Just please don't judge. Stop the looks, the sighs, the under-your-breath comments. As a parent, it makes you feel even worse. It makes that whole situation harder and it's hard not to take it personally. When she's having a bad day we stay home. We just don't go out. Or when she's had it and is about to have a meltdown, at a restaurant or in a store, we all make a mad dash for the car.

How old was Ambryn when she joined your family? And when did you start noticing her uniqueness?

MOM: Ambryn joined our family when she was two days old. I started noticing her uniqueness when she was between nine months and a year old. I do realize that each child is different, but compared to our two older children, she wasn't even close developmentally, especially with her gross motor skills.

DAD: The diagnosis was a huge surprise for me. I was in complete denial. Even after the diagnosis, I thought that she was just different, because each child is different. I absolutely refused to believe it. It was very hard for me, because you never want to think that anything is wrong with your kids. It's something else that you have to deal with and life is hard enough.

It often seems like one of the parents, the mom or the dad, has more trouble accepting the diagnosis. One gets it and one can't handle it. I was the one who couldn't handle it. It took me at least a year before I could even say the word autism. It took a couple years before I could come to terms with it. I finally did, but it took a long time. I had to go through grieving the loss of the child that she's never going to be. It took a long time for me.

MOM: Now when I look at Ambryn I couldn't imagine it any differently. Would I take it back? I don't know if I'd take it back but I wish I would have been more knowledgeable. I lacked a lot of patience. I knew something was wrong but didn't know what it was. So there is a lot of guilt. But when I look at her and what she's given us I can't imagine it any other way. She has opened our eyes with how she sees the world. Her imagination and her observations are just amazing.

What would you like to tell parents who have a newly diagnosed child?

MOM: When you first get the diagnosis, you don't know what it means for your child. Everything is so new. When she was first diagnosed, if someone had told us that she would be able to, for instance, ask questions two years from then, we would have been skeptical. Or if they told us that she would eventually stop crying every night, we probably wouldn't have believed them. The fear that parents have about whether or not their child would ever do this or that is understandable.

DAD: We still don't know who she's going to be when she's eighteen. It's the unknown that's hard.

MOM: It's good for new parents to know that they're not alone. At the time you think you're absolutely the only one going through whatever emotion you're feeling. But somebody has already gone through it and it's ok to feel whatever you are going through. You're not alone. It can be helpful for new parents to find someone who they can relate to and who understands. We didn't have any friends that knew anything about autism. When she was newly diagnosed we just kept to ourselves. It's hard to talk about it at first. It would have helped to reach out.

DAD: It would be helpful if the experienced parents could be aware of and seek out the new parents, maybe through their child's school. The new parents might not be able to ask for help on their own. Also, it's good for new parents to know that it will get better. It will be hard, but it will get better.

— JOSHUA —
7 YEARS | 5 MONTHS

It's basically just that Joshua's mind works in different ways... He might not understand everything, but for sure he has a sense of connection... He is very mellow and very affectionate. That's his best trait, his affection.

Joshua's mom

— JOSHUA —

What would you like people to know about your son?

MOM: Joshua still needs twenty-four hour supervision from us. He cannot think on his own. He doesn't have a sense of safety, except for basic things, like he knows that if he stepped off the couch he would fall. He only uses one hand when eating so he needs assistance. It's basically just that Joshua's mind works in different ways. He is sensitive to sounds. He still flaps his hands.

With Josh the communication is very different. He holds my hand and brings me to what he wants. He's still communicating. It's just how you look at it. It seems like they all connect in some way. Some autistic kids might not like to be touched, but they connect in different ways. Josh totally connects with us. He connects with his family members by holding hands. Joshua might not understand everything, but for sure he has a sense of connection.

We were playing scrabble yesterday, and he participated by putting all the tiles back into the bag. He has improved so much. Those are my little joys. Any little improvement just makes my day. I don't expect a lot from him. I just hope and pray that he reaches his maximum capacity, whatever that is. We just want him to be comfortable and happy. I'm not really asking for a lot but I know God gave me this special child for a reason. I don't know what it is exactly, but I'm happy to have him and to care for him. The most important thing is for him to be comfortable and for him to know that his family loves him.

What is Joshua's best trait?

MOM: He is very mellow and very affectionate. That's his best trait, his affection. He loves to cuddle and hug. I often hear people say that kids with autism don't like to be touched. But it's different with him.

He's better now at listening to me when I tell him not to do something. He has more self-control. He's really trying his best. When he gets in trouble he knows it and he'll run to me. I'll say, "Josh, what did you do? Joshie, that's not good." And then he'll go on the couch and put his hand over his head and be really quiet. He'll just stay there. Later, I'll give him a big hug.

And what are his favorite things to do? What makes him happy?

MOM: The thing that he loves the most is water. He loves the faucet. He's continually turning it on and off. He gets really excited at bath time. He can undress himself now and put his clothes in the bin. He knows how to take off his diaper and put it in the trash. Then he jumps into the tub. He loves water. Every time my husband waters the yard, Joshua likes to get wet. He loves going swimming. He loves pools. He'll jump from the stairs and swim to me. It's O.K. if we're nearby. He loves water.

He also loves anything that swivels, like the sit-n-spin. He likes to make it spin fast and watch it or touch it. He likes to press buttons. He loves to play with balloons. Joshua likes to open and close doors. He likes the noise it makes. Ever since he was little he would squeeze himself into a little closet and close the door. I think the squeezing gives him comfort. He has a favorite blanket. It literally entertains him. He's had it ever since he was little. He likes to throw it around. He's not so attached that it gets in the way of anything. He doesn't miss it when it's not around. It's only when he sees it that he really plays with it.

He is really happy when he is outdoors, like in the park. He loves to run. He loves swinging. We go to the beach a lot. He loves the feel of the waves on his feet. If I don't hold him he'd just dive into the water. He loves the sand, because he likes to pour it. He has a little trolley that my husband attaches to his bike when we go riding. As long as he's outside, he's happy.

We did have an incident, when he was about two, which totally broke my heart. We were in a restaurant and I couldn't control his screaming. Sometimes he just likes to make loud noises. A parent at a nearby table was looking at us with a really mean expression, like, "Why can't you control your son!" We were still eating and I was trying to quiet Josh. Finally, I took him outside to walk. While we were on our way out, the parent said something really mean, like, "You need to control your kids. We're trying to have a nice dinner here." They said that they understood because they had kids at home. I said, "No, you do not understand. He's a different kid. He is not a typical child. He's a special child. He is autistic. So you do not understand." And then I walked out. I was so mad. I felt so bad.

We did have a nice experience with someone from the community. Joshua's sister is on a swimming team. While she's swimming I sit with Josh, holding him, reading to him, trying to keep him occupied. One of the school staff came and said, "Hi Josh, how are you?" He asked if he could take Josh for a walk. I told him, "Oh, he has autism." And he said, "Yes, I know. I volunteer in a program that works with kids like him." It felt good to have Josh understood. I'm very protective. I don't want people wondering what he's doing and thinking that he's weird. It feels good when people actually approach him, and take him by the hand, and are really kind to him, because they know. It feels like you belong. It can be difficult.

Anything that can help the public understand helps the parents and children. Most people have no idea of what we go through every day with a child with autism. It's tough. If you asked me what can be done to make it easier for parents who are raising kids with autism, I'd say "awareness and understanding." It is just as simple as that. When you go to the grocery store or to a restaurant or to a park, just be more welcoming. Just be understanding with everyone. Not just only people with autism. With anyone who is at all different.

— JOSIE —
7 YEARS | 3 MONTHS

I would describe Josie as free-spirited. She can be wild and very
silly. Her humor is contagious. She can also be fearful, hesitant,
as well as very stubborn. There are many doors in her.

Josie's mom

– JOSIE –

What would you like people to know about Josie?

MOM: I'd like the world to know that she is fun-loving. She's smart. She has her own view of things and she makes really keen observations. She thinks things through. She watches everything before she participates. She has recently become much more inquisitive. In the past, she wasn't asking as many questions because she had less language. Now that she has better ability to conceptualize, she has a wider range of questions. You get to see more into her mind. She's very interesting. I would describe Josie as free-spirited. She can be wild and very silly. Her humor is contagious. She can also be fearful, hesitant, as well as very stubborn. There are many doors in her.

What does Josie do really well? What are her strengths and talents?

MOM: She's a good reader. She likes to read. She's good at sounding out words, decoding, and spelling words.

JOSIE: A good writer.

MOM: Yeah, you can write really well. She's in first grade. Next year she'll be in second.

Josie is very thoughtful when it comes to people. She notices things and she has a good memory. My mom uses artificial sweeteners. In the past when we would go to restaurants Josie would collect them for her Grandma.

Josie is also a very good big sister. She helps watch her little sister and will tell me if her baby sister is trying to get out of her high chair or if she's eating something she's not supposed to. She likes to play with her. She gets down on the ground and crawls around with her.

Does Josie have friends at school?

MOM: When she was little and we first started going to the playground, all the kids would play together, and she'd be off on her own. And all the mothers would gather together, and I'd be off on my own. We were both off on our own.

Now, Josie has friends at school. One of her friends lives down the street and he comes over sometimes. It's mostly parallel play, with each of them doing their own thing, but they like being around each other. He's on the spectrum as well. I think he likes her pirate ships. She also has a friend that she likes to visit. I used to worry that she was just there for the toys. I felt bad about that until her neighborhood friend started doing the same thing. So I thought that it must be okay.

What services is she receiving. What approaches are you using?

MOM: She's been getting OT and speech at a local clinic for the past few years. It's amazing how much progress she's made. I have a picture of her at Lake Erie sitting on the sand with both feet in the air, because she could not put them on the sand. Now she can stand on the sand and play in the water. Small things like that help us see how far she's traveled.

We started the full biomedical approach about three months ago. We had been doing the gluten/casein-free diet for about a year. We had tried it when she was younger, but hadn't seen much difference. This time, we started to see notable differences after about four months. We were on vacation, and for the first time were able to actually have a conversation. That was a good day. The good days really stick out in your mind. We were in a store, having what you'd call a normal mother/daughter conversation. It was amazing.

And what is she still working on, still developing?

MOM: Communication. The way she talks. She's had a lot of language growth over the last six months. When she was in preschool if I asked her "How was your day?" I would get no response. Then later she might say a one word answer like, "Bus" or "Teacher" or "Good." And If I asked, "What did you do?" she'd say, "Good." She wasn't really listening to what I was asking. About nine or ten months ago, she started to give longer more appropriate answers. The first time she answered with more information, I was amazed. It was huge. She could finally understand questions and formulate answers. It's so nice to be able to have a conversation with her. She is still working. Her speech is much more understandable. We're working on her ability to initiate and continue conversations, and socialize with other kids.

– JOSIE –

One day last summer we were meeting some friends at the beach. It took a long time to gather and pack up everything, sit through traffic, and finally arrive at the beach. I was carrying the baby, the diaper bag, the lunch bag, beach towels, all the sand toys and keeping track of Josie. It felt like it took forever to get to our friends on the beach. When we finally got to them, Josie had to go to the bathroom. She didn't want to go to the public toilet, so she ended up going all over herself. I had to change her. Then later she had to go again. This time I was able to get her to the public bathroom, but she was screaming and having a tantrum the whole time. Then the baby started crying. It was crazy. Finally, I just said, "We have to go." We had been there for maybe a half an hour. I was driving home thinking, "That was just wasted effort." Later that night when I was putting her to bed, I said, "Good night Josie, I love you." It was the same thing I said every single night as I put her down. That night she actually said, "I love you, Mom." Now, I remember that day as one of the best days of my life. All the hassle, everything that had gone wrong, doesn't matter at all because that was the day that Josie said, "I love you, Mom."

I'd like people to know that autism is not all that she is. It's just a word. It's just a diagnosis or a label. A label can be pretty static. It describes her in some ways, but it's not all that she is. And she's constantly changing. You have to appreciate every little thing. They become huge. And they are. I think that is something I've learned being in a family with autism. Before the diagnosis these milestones would have seemed like no big deal. But, with Josie, every new step becomes monumental.

— AUGUST —
7 YEARS | 0 MONTHS

We're very tuned into all the little successes...
A while back he smiled when I picked him up from school. I realized
that, up until then, he didn't usually smile when I picked him up from
school. It was a big deal that he was happy to see me.

August's mom

– AUGUST –

What would you like to tell me about your son?

MOM: August has a great sense of humor. The older he gets, the more it comes out. He tries to make jokes or be silly with us at home, in private. It's in there. It's slowly coming out. And he's developed a kind of mischievous personality. He likes to push the edge of the envelope a little bit, in a joking way. He'll walk past me, pick up something, and try to hide it behind his back. I can clearly see it, while he's trying to sneak away. It's really funny to see.

August is the most coordinated kid you will ever want to meet. He just learned to ride a bicycle. He never needed training wheels. My husband helped him a few times, and that was it. He can also climb up anything. He can climb and maneuver and swing and jump off of things. He likes full body activities, like monkey bars and swing sets. He also likes spectator sports. We've taken him to sports games. He'll sit and watch the whole thing. I don't know how much he understands, but he just sits and watches and he's fine. He got used to the loud sounds, like all of the cheering. At first he would cover his ears but then he got accustomed to it.

What is he still learning and developing?

MOM: The hardest thing for him is the social, but he tries. He's come a long way from when he first got diagnosed. He can verbally express whatever he wants, but he chooses not to. He doesn't use words all the time, but he has the capacity to speak. It comes and goes. He'll sound just like the other kids. He uses phrases appropriately that he's heard the other kids say. He'll say "That's mine" or "Put that back" or "I said don't talk to me right now." That was the line he said in the car recently because he was busy playing. It's coming slowly.

He's learning play skills. He likes to play with action figures. With other kids he wants to be a part of it, you can tell, but he just doesn't know how to join in. A friend of mine has a son who is older than Augie, and she told him to look out for Augie. Now that's his personal mission.

– AUGUST –

Wherever he goes he brings Augie with him. He can get Augie to do things. He'll say, "Okay now we're going to sit down and eat," and Augie will sit down and eat. But generally the social is really hard for Augie. When he plays with others he tries a little bit, but it's still more like parallel play, where he's imitating what they're doing. It's come a long way but he's still working on that.

Does he have to have thousands of friends? No. He's got his family and that's what is really important. If he has one really good friend then I'm okay with that. We used to work hard on the play skills and try to make him fit in. What I discovered is that kids are nicer than people think. His classmates are nice.

They make sure to include him in everything. And the little boys help him do things. I saw one little boy say to him "Augie he said hi. Turn around and say hi to him." So, Augie turned around and said hi. The kids have a great capacity for acceptance. I was at his school with our oldest daughter and she was shocked at the number of kids that said hi to Augie as we walked by. I said, "Did you know that your brother was so popular?" She said "I'm shocked." He knows all of his classmates. He might not say "Hi" or "Goodbye" right away, because he's not really focused. But if we tap him on the shoulder and point it out, he'll respond.

The other kids at school look out for him. The boys that are rougher aren't bothered at all if he bumps into them or does something that's rough. They just keep going. There was a boy in his kindergarten class that always made sure that Augie got his spot. He would say, "This is his spot next to me." The kids look out for him. They help him get in line when the bell rings. They'll say, "Augie, you're supposed to be right here." They look out for him. They've always done that. They are really good with him.

How does he do out in the community?

MOM: He is a lot better out in public. He used to just take off, so it was hard to take him anywhere. Now it's easier to go places with him. When he was younger people would always want to engage him, and he would not respond or he would turn away. I used to think, "Please don't speak to him." It was embarrassing because he was not going to respond to them. Someone would come up and say "Hey, little fellow. What's going on?" And his head would be all the way in the corner of the stroller because he didn't want to speak. It's better now. If someone says hi, I tell him to say hi, and he'll generally go along with the flow. It's good for the public to realize that generally kids don't do things to be purposely bad, whether they have autism or not. I wish people would realize that kids can't always help themselves. I think August is a wonderful kid but not everybody is going to see that and I've just had to let that go, which is better because it was making me crazy.

What are some recent successes that you'd like to share?

MOM: We're very tuned into all the little successes. There's always something new. A while back he smiled when I picked him up from school. I realized that, up until then, he didn't usually smile when I picked him up from school. It was a big deal that he was happy to see me. Little things are big successes. Making it through the entire school day without having a fit or being aggressive is a big success. You really learn to appreciate the little things. Although they are not little. They're huge but it's just a little bit every day, instead of these giant leaps. Every once in a while you get a giant leap. But a lot of the time it's just little bitty steps. You're happy for each and every one because you think that four years ago you never thought we'd be here. It's going to be okay. No matter how it turns out, it will be okay. And that's how it is with me.

— ETHAN —
7 YEARS | 9 MONTHS

Ethan has really good memory for events and conversations. He can quote back to you pretty much exactly the way things were said. It's helpful for him because sometimes he's kind of a lawyer about following the rules.

Ethan's dad

– ETHAN –

What would you like to tell me about your middle son, Ethan?

DAD: When Ethan was younger he had articulation problems.

MOM: His speech was a little slow to develop, but his articulation was so bad that it could have been that we just didn't understand him. It is hard to say. A lot of the places don't like to diagnose high-functioning autism or Asperger's, until after the child is at least six years old. He originally had a diagnosis of pervasive developmental disorder (PDD). We took him back after he was six and they diagnosed him as high-functioning autism. They told us that the only difference between Asperger's and high-functioning autism is that with high-functioning autism they had a speech delay and with Asperger's they didn't.

DAD: Ethan is kind of like a little professor type.

MOM: He is a smart guy. When he was about a year old he saw a baby elephant at the zoo and he was hooked. For years we had elephant birthday parties. At about eighteen months old, he was saying that he liked the reticulated giraffes that have a net-like pattern on them. He knew about them because that is the kind that they had at the zoo. He obsessed over those. And he also loved dolphins. And from there his interests grew to include all animals and insects.

During preschool he learned all his letters and they had started teaching him the sounds of the letters. One day, after he had completed preschool, he brought me a Dr. Sues book and asked if I would read it to him. He wasn't quite five yet, probably about four and a half. I had something that I had to do for a few minutes so I said "See if you can put some of the letters together. See if you can figure out what the words are." I came back five minutes later and he was reading it as if he had been reading for years. He just kind of taught himself to read.

DAD: Ethan also has a really good memory for events and conversations. He can quote back to you pretty much exactly the way things were said. It's helpful for him because sometimes he's kind of a lawyer about following the rules.

– ETHAN –

MOM: He's the kid that goes in to the children's play area at a fast food restaurant, reads the rules, and enforces them, although he doesn't tend to follow them all the time himself. For instance, he's usually supposed to wear socks, which he doesn't. They're kind of uncomfortable for him.

When he was younger, he wanted so much to make friends. We'd be somewhere, and he didn't know how to approach other kids. So he'd go up to them, follow them around and giggle and laugh oddly around them. He'd then end up yelling or screaming or something. This worked great when he wanted the attention of his classroom aides. But the kids would be afraid and they'd run off. Eventually he did learn how to make friends

DAD: You hear that people with autism have a hard time with physical contact, that you shouldn't touch them, and that they need a lot of personal space. I am sure that is true of some people with autism but it's not true with our kids[14] at all. They don't have aversions as much as they have cravings for sensory input. It's different with them.

MOM: People are so nervous. When I try to bring up things about my kids to moms of typical kids, you can kind of see them bristle, because they don't know how to approach it. It makes them nervous. I think that it's just a lack of education. I love to talk about my kids. Some of it's hard and some of it's good. But I love my kids and I love to talk about them. I understand the bristling reaction because I had such a lack of education about special needs before my kids educated me. I think that if we can give people just five or ten minutes of simple education it can help immensely. To let them know that these are people who have a harder time making human contact. We can learn from these special needs kids, because they bring such a sense of tolerance. It could make such a huge difference in our world today if we could just learn some tolerance, instead of all the fighting.

---

14   Our kids: Ethan, Rowan, page 46, and Ayden, page 134

– ETHAN –

DAD: It is all related, because whenever people are different we start categorizing and segregating them into groups. The practical result is that everybody gets to know only that which is the same and familiar. When you grow up like that you're only accustomed to what you're familiar with. Then when you're confronted with something that's different, it makes you feel uncomfortable. You're afraid of it, and you don't know what to do with it. A lot of times people become angry or afraid. There are parallels. If we segregate kids with special needs from typical kids, then the typical kids often tend to make fun of them or are mean to them. They don't have experience with them so they don't know how to deal with them. The same thing happens with adults. When a culture isolates itself for a long time, and then they get exposed to another culture, they tend to become warlike because they feel threatened.

— EIGHT TO TEN YEARS —

When Ayden was diagnosed, I was actually glad to get his diagnosis, because it meant that I wasn't insane and I wasn't a horrible mother. It was a relief to have some help with him and I desperately needed it. But once that diagnosis came I wondered, "Were does the autism end and my son begin." – Ayden's mom

Some people don't know what autism is. Some people think it's being crazy or flapping your hands, or things like that. I don't want people to look at him like he's crazy or something. Some people think he's acting the way he does because he's spoiled. He's not spoiled. He's special.

– ~~Ayden's mom~~ – Majeed's mom

I don't only dwell on what she can't do. I also recognize what she can do. She's interested in things that a lot of typical girls are. She likes the same music and movies, which gives her something to talk about when she's with other girls her age, and they can see that she's not that different, that she likes the same things that they like.

– Jessica's mom

When you say you have an autistic daughter, some people will ask you questions, to try to understand it, and some people just move away or change the subject. I just go wherever they go, because if they're not asking, I'm not giving them any information. That's my experience. If they ask me questions, I'm open to telling them whatever they want to know. But if they don't ask me any questions, we'll just move on to something else. Some people want to hear about it, some people don't.

– Ronnie's dad

— MAJEED —
8 YEARS | 3 MONTHS

We get excited every time he says or does something new...
He's not always aware of what's going on around him. But every once in
a while he will have a day where he's very aware and notices everything.

Majeed's mom

How would you describe Majeed?

MOM: Majeed is a quiet, shy boy. It's hard to know what's inside, because he doesn't always have the communication to let us know, though his language is much better now.

DAD: In the past, when I called from overseas, he would push the phone away. But recently he really talked to me.

MOM: We get excited every time he says or does something new. He's reading better than last year. Some of the words he's memorized, but he will also try to sound out the words that he doesn't know. He's not always aware of what's going on around him. But every once in a while he will have a day where he's very aware and notices everything. On other days it's hard to get his attention.

PERWANA (older sister): He goes through these fads. For a while he was cutting or ripping out tiny pictures. He'd cry and we'd have to search the house if he lost any of them. Then he started drawing pictures. Every day he'd use up a stack of papers. He's really good at drawing.

MOM: But now he doesn't like drawing anymore. Now he wants to play on the computer or with the video games. This morning he put some gel on his hair. When asked why he did that, he said it was to be like his favorite musical group. He's different from moment to moment, day to day. He'll make different choices, even with his food. For a couple of weeks he will like one food, and then he'll stop eating it. We have to struggle to find out what he likes next.

He doesn't like eating. When he's told that he has to eat he often says, "It's not eating time." He still needs to be fed. He can eat some finger food by himself if he likes it. Otherwise, if he's left to himself he will just sit there and look at the food. Or he'll leave the table.

He knows streets. He can't read the street signs, but if we're in our neighborhood, or another familiar place, he knows where we are going.

DAD: If we're driving to someplace familiar, like to his school, or to the clinic, he can tell where we are going. He loves the clinic where he gets OT and speech. He gets very happy when we are getting near the area.

– MAJEED –

MOM: Majeed has had sleep problems since he was very young. He used to wake up in the middle of the night and laugh. He'd be laughing and laughing. We'd wonder what he was laughing about. And then we'd start laughing too. Every night he would be laughing. Sometimes he would suddenly scream loudly and then laugh, just for fun.

When he was little he liked to put all his small toys in a long line. Sometimes he would even put the videocassettes in a line. We didn't know why he did that. At the time we didn't know that he had autism. We didn't know what autism was. We had never heard of it. He was about three years old when he was diagnosed. That's when we found out that what he was doing was common in children with autism.

Majeed is sensitive to some sounds. But then other times, he'll put his ear on the TV and turn it up really loud. His teacher said that sometimes he puts his ear on the loud speaker. Maybe he likes the vibration. He's different from moment to moment.

DAD: He's very good with the other kids. He wouldn't harm anybody. He's very good.

MOM: He doesn't have tantrums. Occasionally, he will cry, like any kid. But he doesn't tantrum. At school he's mostly by himself. The other kids will be playing on the jungle gym and swings, while he'll be walking around the outside of the playground, playing with very small stones. Every day when he comes home his hands are very dirty and he has a lot of dirt on his face. I asked the teacher what is going on and why his hands are always so dirty. She said that no matter what she does, he just wants to play on the edge of the playground with the small stones.

PERWANA: He used to be really shy and quiet with people. Now he's a little more social with me and our brother. He's also louder now and not so quiet. He's more playful.

What do you play together?
PERWANA: We have different games we play. He likes "hide and seek" but he gets tired of it. I'll tell him to count to ten while I hide. But instead of trying to find me, he'll come into the room and call out my name. He expects me to answer him and then he finds me by my voice. There's another game we call "Lion." I sit on the bed and when he tries to get on I growl at him and he runs away. Then he pretends to get me and he gets on the bed.

He had to learn a joke for his social skills group, so I taught him, "Knock, knock." "Who's there?" "Boo." "Boo who?" "Do not cry, it's just a joke." It was hard to teach him. But he really liked it and kept saying it.

MOM: Sometimes he says something he thinks is funny and then he looks at us. Even if it's not funny we have to say, "Ha ha! That was funny."

Do you think he likes to see people's reactions?
PERWANA: Yeah.

People can make assumptions about autism. If someone knew that Majeed has autism but had not met him yet, what would you want them to know about him?
MOM: Some people don't know what autism is. Some people think it's being crazy or flapping your hands, or things like that. I don't want people to look at him like he's crazy or something. Some people think he's acting the way he does because he's spoiled. He's not spoiled. He's special.

DAD: To be honest, it's going to bother us; it's going to hurt us. And some autistic children that you see are much better than the typical kids in the school these days. You see typical kids doing things like hitting other kids. Majeed doesn't do that kind of thing. Whatever he does, he does by himself and it's not going to affect anyone else. It's okay.

— JORDAN —

8 YEARS | 4 MONTHS

A lot of things about Jordan are atypical of what you would normally
think of someone with autism. She wants human interaction. She's
very empathetic. She gets very distressed when somebody else is sad or
angry. She's really in-tune with other people's emotions.

Jordan's dad

How would you describe Jordan?

MOM: Jordan is not typical in terms of what people think about kids with autism. We stay away from people who want to treat her as if she fits a cookie-cutter definition. Jordan is extremely intelligent. She is very aware of her surroundings and what's going on. She's a very sweet and loving soul. She's also reserved, cautious and very sensitive.

Jordan is in a typical second-grade classroom at a wonderful school. The teachers are very loving and accepting. They see her for who she is. They see her sense of humor. They recognize and appreciate her intelligence. Her teacher told me that the kids adore her. If we're walking around in public and a little kid comes up and gives Jordan a hug, we know it's a kid from her school.

She was in the school play. It was her first big play in the school auditorium, with full scenery and costumes. She did a good job. She knew her part. She knew where she was supposed to be.

DAD: She knew everyone's parts. Jordan has had speech therapy and occupational therapy as part of her school day. She also gets OT at a private sensory integration clinic. She's still working on certain self-help skills. Her fine motor control needs some work. Her gross motor is fine.

MOM: Jordan is probably a gifted kid. By the time she was two, she knew the ABCs, she knew numbers, and she knew some words in different languages, at least to the degree that we understood. She wrote DOG when she was about two. However, there wasn't a whole lot of language.

DAD: Jordan has a very good memory. A while back we were talking about a sheep dog and she said, "Scottish Low Land Sheep Dog or an Old English Sheep Dog?" She's great at writing her own stories. She has great imagination. She could be a playwright. She is our DJ. She loves music. She has quite a sense of humor. She'll say that she fell down and saw birds flying around her head or saw stars flying around her head, like in the cartoons. When our rabbit died she said that he had Xs on his eyes.

MOM: She takes weekly private ballet lessons and piano lessons. She's in a piano recital later today. She's also very good at taking care of her brother and sister, if they don't feel very well or they need support or she thinks Mommy and Daddy are too harsh on them.

Do you have any advice for parents of children who are just getting diagnosed with ASD[15]?

MOM: It's important for parents to know that there is a whole lot of support. Right now we're also trying to take advantage of some of the newer holistic-type approaches that are available. We're seeing results. The approaches make sense. The techniques are incorporated into our home life. Our doctor told us, "Don't treat a diagnosis. If there's an issue that you need to work on, work on that issue. Stay away from just treating a label."

While many therapies are based on behavior modification, we've been using RDI, Relational Developmental Intervention, which is much more about remediation. You're helping to connect what's not connected. You're teaching the child to be more naturally dynamic, and less rote. A lot of people assume that just because they can't understand the child's communication, it's not there. We pressure the child with autism to be able to communicate in our world, in our language, but we're not making any effort to communicate with the child in their world, in their language.

Jordan's early intervention program stressed not flapping her arms. But then she just switched to rocking her head. So, we just let her flap. When she would say off-the-wall things, they would say, "That's not appropriate. Stay on topic." We didn't feel comfortable with that because that was her way of communicating. We can use what she said and bring it in to a conversation. So, we chose to stop the behavioral approach. We've decided to go another route and let her be herself. Before that we were only working on her weaknesses.

---

15   ASD: Autism Spectrum disorder

Do you think some people, when they hear that your daughter has autism, might make assumptions about her?

DAD: Jordan is not just stuck in her own world. She seeks interaction with others. A lot of things about Jordan are atypical of what you would normally think of someone with autism. She wants human interaction. She's very empathetic. She gets very distressed when somebody else is sad or angry. She's really in tune with other people's emotions.

MOM: Her level of communication is a lot better. Now she works a lot more on getting engagement and making sure you're paying attention.

DAD: It's happened more naturally than the rote methods she had learned. It's just evolved over time.

MOM: We've had to tell people that are around her to stop asking her to look at them. Don't try to force her to look at you. Just carry on as though she's listening. When we watch our other kids, they don't continually look at us. They occasionally glance. That has been much more effective with Jordan. There is so much going on that it might be easier for her to look away as a means to manage her ability to pay attention to what you're saying.

DAD: She just took part in a Special Olympics track meet. Jordan has no competitive spirit. It doesn't make any difference to her whether she comes in first or last. The whole idea of trying to beat somebody in a race is really foreign to her. She's not one to push herself very hard. The only way that she would practice hard was if it was made into a game. We'd pretend to be Tweety Bird and Sylvester, and then she'd run like crazy. She's really fast. But if you put her on the track by herself and tell her to run as fast as she can, she'll run a little, but then just slow down and look around. She needs some motivation. In some ways it's kind of good, because the competitive spirit can get to be extreme in a negative way.

— TIMMY —

8 YEARS | 4 MONTHS

Timmy is very outgoing ...
He definitely wants to connect with people ...
He's still trying to learn how to do it, but he is very outgoing.

Timmy's mom

– TIMMY –

How would you describe Timmy's personality?

DAD: Timmy is a very smart boy. He could learn to be more sympathetic. Part of the reason he needs to learn to be more sympathetic is because people tease him so much, or misunderstand him, at school, in public, at church, in the neighborhood, everywhere. He's going to have to learn to be more flexible. But he's a good boy. He's good-natured. He wants to do good things.

MOM: Timmy is very outgoing. He wants to socialize. I know that a lot of children with autism don't want that. He definitely wants to connect with people. I really feel blessed about that. He's still trying to learn how to do it, but he is very outgoing. He has a sense of humor. He's very gentle.

What are Timmy's strengths?

MOM: Timmy's very good with driving directions. I've never seen anyone do so well with directions. His memory is phenomenal. A friend of mine lives quite a distance from us. We haven't been to her house for about three years and he still knows the exit to take. He's very good with directions. Another thing about Timmy is that once he knows that a rule is set in stone and it's not going to budge, then he will uphold it himself to the nth degree. For instance, he's into signs and posted rules, like "no smoking," "no guns," "no dogs." We were at the local aquarium. There was a "no smoking" sign. This guy came walking by smoking a cigarette. Timmy went up to him and he said, "No smoking," and took the cigarette right out of his mouth. The guy said, "I guess this is a sign I should give up smoking."

DAD: Timmy is very fact-based.

MOM: And he's going to uphold the rules.

What are his favorite things to do?

MOM: Timmy's favorite things are the trampoline and the bike. He taught himself how to ride a two wheel bike without training wheels. He taught himself how to swim. He likes movement. And we do a lot of sensory activities. We wrap him up in a blanket and then jump with him on the trampoline. He just loves that. At night we also try to wrap him up real tight in his blankets, which seems to help him with his sleeping. He's all snug.

– TIMMY –

How is he at school?

MOM: We had tried to mainstream him. Kindergarten went alright, because kindergarten was just half a day and they were very flexible if he had an outburst or something. They had a corner he could go to and calm down. In first grade, he did okay for a few months, and then it got progressively worse. When we tried to mainstream him into second grade, it was just a complete, total failure. He was in a huge class. He couldn't handle all the noise. Timmy has very, very sensitive hearing. Most of his sensitivities have to do with tactile and hearing.

DAD: He would run out of the school, and there were two busy streets nearby.

MOM: Now he's in an enclosed class. There are only seven students in the class, which is really good for him. He also seems to have obsessive compulsive disorder. He hasn't been diagnosed with it. In September he's going to see a neurologist. I'm hoping that they're going to figure out what else is affecting his learning besides autism. He's not reading yet.

DAD: He might be dyslexic.

How are other children with him?

DAD: Sometimes the typical kids at his school copy him. "Copy" means mock. They mock him.

MOM: He usually connects with children that are younger than him. There's a little boy at church that he's really good friends with. He's not autistic but he has sensory integration issues too. They're the kids that you can hear yelling in the back of the church, because either someone's touched them or there's some loud noise or something else that sets them off. When we hear a kid yelling, we know it's either Timmy or his friend.

How is it when you're out in the community?

MOM: There are some people that are understanding and are helpful. Once when Timmy was little, he was tantrumming on the floor of a store. Other mothers walked by and gave looks, like

"My kid doesn't do that." I could tell by their expressions. And then this one older woman came over and said, "I'm so sorry this is happening to you." She said, "Actually, my daughter has a child who has this problem. My grandson is autistic." I said, "Yeah, he is too." She said, "I could tell." And then she said, "Just ignore everybody else. Just try to settle this. The more you get worried about what other people are thinking, the more the child will read into it." She said, "If you can just calm yourself down, that will probably help him to calm down." And she was right.

What strategies have worked for you in raising Timmy?

DAD: I want to tell you what we were doing wrong. It's good for other parents to hear. We learned from the support group that one of the things that we did wrong, especially me, is that I would get too mad at him. I would yell at him and that doesn't work. It does not work. One of the techniques we learned from other parents is praising him when he does it right.

Most of the credit goes to my wife, for figuring out all this and reading everything she could. She really stepped up and said, "Hey, something's wrong here" and got him diagnosed.

MOM: When I'm totally frustrated and at the end of my rope, Timmy's dad has done a lot of what I would call the occupational therapy here at home. He does a lot of the sensory activities with Timmy. He's also taught Timmy to do things that I just don't have the patience to teach him.

DAD: She is a very good mother, very good for Timmy.

— JESSICA —
8 YEARS | 6 MONTHS

Jessica is very charming... even though she is a child with challenges and obstacles to overcome. She can give other people happiness just with her smile. People seem drawn to something in her spirit.

Jessica's mom

– JESSICA –

How would you describe Jessica's personality?

MOM: Jessica is very charming. People have told me that seeing her smile lightened their spirit when they were having a bad day. Even though she is a child with challenges and obstacles to overcome, she can give other people happiness just with her smile. I think she inspires hope. People seem drawn to something in her spirit. Jessica can also sense if a person is good or not. Everyone has a purpose in this world. Each person has their own unique gifts. Here's a child who has so many challenges, but she doesn't give up and she's still so happy.

What does she enjoy doing?

MOM: Recently she's gotten really good at coloring and she loves to do it. She's very detailed and very particular about what color she wants to use for each section. She also really likes music. For many years she had such little speech that she couldn't sing along. But now she can sing along and she remembers most of the lyrics.

She really likes swimming. She could be in the water all day. She likes to go to the bottom of the deep end of the pool, and then she pops back up and smiles at me, like she's so proud. She has very good control in the water. Her instructor has been showing her how to use more advanced arm movements, while she's kicking her legs.

What is she still working on or developing?

MOM: She still does some stimming. She has language delay and she also has sensory issues. She used to not like to touch different materials and textures. She's slowly coming out of that, although there are still times when she doesn't want to touch something, or if it's a new food she doesn't want to try it. She still has sensitivities to different noises. She'll cover her ears or tighten up all over if there's too much noise.

Her speech has improved so much over the past few years. Before she was mostly just pointing and saying one or two words. She'd say, "Eat, eat," or "Go home, go home," or "No no." Now she's asking full questions, like, "Where are we going?" or "What are we doing next?" or "Why are you doing that?" She asks, "Why?" a lot, which is typical for kids.

She has friends at school. She just started spending part of her school day in a mainstream class. A little girl in her new class gave her a note that says, "You are my friend." Jessica enjoys telling me about her friends at school.

I don't only dwell on what she can't do. I also recognize what she can do. She's interested in things that a lot of typical girls are. She likes the same music and movies, which gives her something to talk about when she's with other girls her age, and they can see that she's not that different, that she likes the same things that they like. She likes video games. It has been a good way to connect with other children. They'll talk about what games they have.

A lot of her traits are age appropriate. Her cousin is going to be in a quinceañera of a friend, which in the Mexican culture is a big celebration for a girl's fifteenth birthday. In preparation, she's going to weekly dancing classes and she takes Jessica with her to every class. My sister was telling me that Jessica is so social there. In the Latin culture when you say hello, you also give the person a kiss on the cheek. She told me that at dance class, Jessica says hello and gives a kiss to everyone. And she's learned all the dance steps. That's another one of her talents. She loves to dance. She likes some of the Spanish dance music, and she likes hip-hop because her twelve year old cousin is into that. She'll know the name of the songs and a lot of the words. When she hears a favorite song, she starts dancing.

How is she doing in school?

MOM: Jessica is in third grade, but she's mainstreamed in a second grade class. She's not quite up with the other kids. She's had so many challenges with her gross and fine motor skills. Her reading fluency is at the second grade level. Her comprehension skills are a little more delayed. But considering how much difficulty this child has had to go through, for her to be able to read, even at a second grade level, is amazing. The gap is getting smaller. I think she's just now starting to learn. It took years for her to develop her gross motor, fine motor, and speech skills, while most kids do those things at two, three and four years old. It's amazing what she can do now, given all that she's been through.

I couldn't feel more blessed. I know that we're seeing progress. Even though the progress might be slow, it's constant. And she'll have these jumps where all of a sudden she does something new. She might plateau for a while and then she'll advance again. So, I can't ask for more. As far as I'm concerned she doesn't need to go at the same pace as the other kids, as long as she keeps moving forward. She has her own pace.

Even while she was getting speech, OT, PT and ABA, I was constantly on the look out to see what else I could do for her. I wanted to give her the opportunity to be the best that she could be. I had heard about and researched dolphin therapy and how it could help kids with autism. We found a program in Mexico that was more affordable. The next time we went to visit family in Mexico we also went there. When we came back our friends, and some of her therapists, immediately noticed differences. She made better eye contact and when people talked to her she turned toward them and was actually paying attention to them. There was the sense that she was connected to the world. It just seemed like a lot of things started fitting together.

If someone knew that your daughter has autism, but hadn't met her yet, what would you want them to know, beyond the possible assumptions about autism?

MOM: I want people to know that Jessica is very lovable and loving. She helps us realize that we all have a purpose in this life and that we all have things we're working toward. It's important not to get all involved in the material things of this world, and envy others for the things that they have. It's important to realize that life is very simple and sometimes what we tend to think is very important is not. You have to look and see the person's inner self. When people tell me, "Your child made me so happy today," it reinforces for me the connection that we all have. It's just that simple. Enjoy that moment. Enjoy all the little life moments.

— ALEXANDER —

8 YEARS | 9 MONTHS

When Alexander was younger I was terrified that his only interest was going to be trains. Then it expanded to the planets, and then to the periodic table. He knows everything about the elements... He's really bright and has a phenomenal memory.

Alexander's mom

– ALEXANDER –

How would you describe Alexander?

MOM: Alexander has classic autism, while his brother Paul[16] has Asperger's. Alexander has a huge heart. He loves everyone and everything. He gets mad at me if I kill a spider or a little ant. He really enjoys watching an ant trail and telling me all about the food chain and all. His favorite things in life are babies and small animals. To see him interact with a baby is so beautiful. He's really gentle. He comes down to their level. It's adorable.

The difference between my boys is their ability or desire to manipulate situations. Alexander doesn't and can't. Although he will manipulate situations by letting people do things for him. He'll use laziness as a manipulation because he knows it will eventually get done somehow. Alexander's not a self-starter. He often has to wait for a prompt.

When did you first have concerns about Alexander?

MOM: Alexander has a regressive form of autism. He was typical until he was twelve months old, walking, talking, playing typically with toys and others. He was doing it all. Then he lost all speech and stopped walking, went back to crawling. It was devastating. I knew something was terribly wrong because you don't just lose skills like that.

Also, his whole first to second year was spent going to tummy specialists because he was always sick. We eventually found out that he had extreme food allergies. After he went off gluten and casein we saw huge improvements. Before that he had been wound up so tight. Every little thing scared him. He practically vibrated. But once we took away the milk he just chilled out. The gluten took a while longer to get rid of because I didn't know that I was giving him hidden gluten, which is in a lot of foods. I had started the diet pretty soon after his second birthday. By his third birthday we had finally gotten all the gluten out of his diet. His language came back right around age three. All of his therapists were just dumbfounded. He went from one to two and three words very quickly. Then he plateaued for a little while.

---

16   Paul, page 68

– ALEXANDER –

We'd had so much difficulty communicating with each other. It was so frustrating because I didn't know what he wanted and he wouldn't want what I offered to him. He had a lot of ABA and was using words as a part of his sessions, but when he was out of therapy he didn't talk. Through his speech therapist we were doing The Listening Program to retrain his auditory processing. He had started getting OT using sensory integration early on. We were able to get him started in therapies pretty early, because he was diagnosed at his two-year-old Well Baby checkup. Finally when he got his speech back we also started PECS, the Picture Exchange Communication System. That helped because then at least he could bring me the picture card of what he wanted. I was just elated when he started talking again. Our household stress level went down significantly. We could finally communicate.

We didn't spend a lot of time in that really dark place. When you and your child don't know how to communicate, it's a really tough place to be. It's not your fault, but it's very frustrating. You start to resent the child because you are doing everything and more, and it's not working. You don't know any better. Once he started to get language back our collective frustration went down.

We learned that Alexander really needed a lot of sensory input throughout the day. He needed lots and lots of movement, so we installed a doorway swing. At first, when he was still having trouble accessing his words the only time he had any words was when he was in the swing. His OT and SLP[17] worked together on the same goals. His speech therapist knew that he needed all the movement and heavy work input, so she would have him on a swing or playing "crashing" type games during speech therapy. The first word that he got back was "go" because he wanted his therapist to swing him. That was phenomenal. He had basic functional language at probably about four years. But it took until about nine years old for him to be able to have actual conversations with us.

Alexander still has his ABA shadow aide at school. He also has school based speech and OT. We're talking about doing a social skills group. I am so blessed to have found the people that I did. Everything just lined up in the right way so that Alexander was able to get better more quickly.

---

17   SLP: Speech-Language Pathologist

− ALEXANDER −

How is he doing in school?

MOM: Academically, he's doing fine. He's been in a general education classroom since he was in second grade. He does daydream a lot though. He is like every other kid, but a little more extreme. He really gets into it. He sees it, feels it, and hears it. He's usually replaying something he's seen on TV or on a video.

Alexander wanted to be a scientist, but he recently had to do a research project. He started to cry one night because it was a tremendous amount of writing. He thought that I was punishing him by making him do the report. I said, "You want to be a scientist, right? Research projects are what scientists do. They research something and then they report on it." He just fell into a puddle of tears. I had broken his heart because he thought that being a scientist was looking through a telescope and discovering new things. He didn't know that there are other steps involved.

How is he with other kids in his class?

MOM: He gets along pretty well with them. They're very interested in him because he's funny and he's good at acting. He is able to exactly copy the sound, tone, and inflection of an actor's voice and the facial expressions. He only has to see it one time. He has good timing and delivery with the jokes. He's funny. So, the kids are interested in him and really like him.

Something that I get hung up on is the stereotypes. Alexander is a typical boy in most ways. He's just autistic. He has similar interests; it's just that with autism they can get stuck on one thing at a time. When Alexander was younger I was terrified that his only interest was going to be trains. Then it expanded to the planets, and then to the periodic table. He knows everything about the elements. He knows where they are on the periodic table, their components and their number. He's really bright and has a phenomenal memory.

— AYDEN —

9 YEARS | 1 MONTH

Ayden was four before he said "mommy." You realize how much more it means than the typical child saying "mommy." Each step along the way is an amazing thing.

Ayden's mom

– AYDEN –

You have three boys who are on the spectrum, Ayden, Rowan and Ethan[18]. How would you describe the oldest, Ayden?

DAD: Ayden is really kind of hot and cold. He has a capacity to be super loving and very good. A lot of the time when we go out, Ayden is the one who behaves the best, and tries to follow the rules.

MOM: It is partly his sensory needs. The visual stimulation when we go out helps to calm him. He's always asking for the radio when we're in the car, so I think that is calming for him. He also calms with tight hugs.

DAD: Ayden is also better than the other kids at doing chores when we ask him. He's eager to please and to help out. On the other hand though, he has times that he'll become uncontrollable with his anxiety or rage. That's the other end of the spectrum. In addition to being very loving, he can be very angry.

MOM: He went through a very aggressive period. He is starting to come out of it, now. I think most of it was communication. It seems like he thinks if he is able to say what he wants, then he should get it. And if he doesn't get it he's mad and he'll show you.

DAD: It's frustrating for him because his language skills are much lower than his other skills. Inside he's processing and he knows what he wants and he just can't get it out. When he gets angry it is not as much external as it is internal. He is upset about something that is going on inside of him. He's got some kind of internal conflict that becomes externalized. He'll sometimes hit or bite, because he's angry that he can't get something that he wants. It's not really that he's angry at someone. It's more about a turmoil that is going on inside. Ayden is also more detached than his brothers. He is not very socially interested.

MOM: Grocery shopping was really hard, especially when I'd had to run in for a few minutes and grab something before he had a melt-down. He would be clawing and hitting at me, while I was trying to go through the line, write the check, and collect the other two. On the way out we would have to stop every other step, while he was trying to get away. I would be on the verge of tears and break down when I finally got in the car.

---

18 Rowan, page 46, and Ethan, page 108

− AYDEN −

At times like that it would have been wonderful if someone could have helped by rounding up the other kids and maybe hold the other kid's hands. One child is an easier problem than three. That was when we were trying to figure out his medications. There were some tough times. But he's definitely doing a lot better now.

We haven't had many people approach us about the kids when we're out in the community. It's usually pretty obvious with Ayden that there is something going on there. Ayden makes a lot of noises and vocalizations. Every now and then someone will ask if he has autism. And then they'll say that they have or they know a child who has autism. We probably don't notice a lot of people's reactions because we are so involved in our own world. We just take the stares and the occasional reactions with a grain of salt. Every once in a while we'll have someone come up to us in a restaurant and say, "Your boys are so good". And I'll say, "Thank you. That means a lot because they have autism and we've worked hard to get them to this point".

When Ayden was diagnosed, I was actually glad to get his diagnosis, because it meant that I wasn't insane and I wasn't a horrible mother. It was a relief to have some help with him and I desperately needed it. But once that diagnosis came I wondered, "Were does the autism end and my son begin." He was assessed to have a non-verbal IQ of 112 and a verbal IQ of 54. We were told that with autism a twenty point difference between those two IQs is more common. We had experts say that having such a big difference is rarely ever seen.

I volunteered in his preschool class. He had an autism specific class with about seven or eight kids in it. It was amazing to see how different they were from Ayden and how each of them were such strong individuals. It's wonderful once you allowed yourself to go into their world and you're able to connect with them. You could see the beauty of it and it meant so much more . Ayden was four before he said "Mommy." You realize how much more it means than the typical child saying "mommy." Each step along the way is an amazing thing.

Ayden used to get pullout time in the typical classrooms. I would talk to the typical classes each year to help educate them. In the beginning of the year the kids would be afraid of him, because he'd make these vocalizations and be loud and for them it was weird. So I went to talk to the class. We talked about the things that Ayden liked. The kids would say, "Oh, I like that too." It gave them a connection to him. Then I'd say, "You know, Ayden has a hard time making friends. He really likes people. But he's got this problem. He thinks differently. His brain doesn't work the same. And that makes it difficult for him to make friends the way he wants to." The kids would say, "If he needs help, I can help him." You could see the switch in how they saw him. It was a beautiful thing.

Some of the teachers saw Ayden's presence in the classroom as an amazing experience, a wonderful possibility, and a teaching opportunity for the kids. And the kids would be just fantastic. One kid raised his hand before I even started and said, "Ayden gave me a hug. It was so cool." Another kid in Ayden's class raised his hand and said that he was learning to use sign language, so he could say hi to a hearing impaired girl in his class. They were so excited about it. It would make such a drastic change, going from the kids looking scared and nervous about the special kids, to seeing them proud to be able to talk and interact with these kids. You could see that they were getting it. The whole class understood what it was to be with kids with special needs and they loved it. The teachers make a huge difference. We need to educate teachers about what an amazing experience it can be to get to know these kids and then it'll get through to the kids.

Unfortunately, in our current school district the more severe kids get sent to a different school, which is a great school but it's kind of sad because they're separated. The kids in our community don't get to know Ayden and they miss out. Because I think it's a wonderful lesson in tolerance and patience. Ayden communicates on a different level than just with speech and it's an amazing thing to learn.

— RONNIE —
9 YEARS | 5 MONTHS

I wish I could get in to her head to see what she's seeing and
hearing and feeling. Most of the time, she's a happy person...
We call it Ronnie's World.

Ronnie's mom

How would you describe Ronnie?

MOM: Our neighbor calls her a free-spirit. I think she's beautiful, smart, determined, hard-headed, but yet very lovable. She gives the best hugs that you'll ever get. And she's funny. She'll joke with her therapist, in her own way. But you don't see that when she's down on the ground throwing a fit. A lot of people never get to see that side of her. A lot of people look at her and think "behavior problem."

I wish I could get in to her head to see what she's seeing and hearing and feeling. Most of the time, she's a happy person, unless she's throwing a fit. Usually, she'll be laughing, giggling, carrying on, and dancing around. We call it Ronnie's World. She dances around a lot. She's a pretty happy kid.

When she tantrums it's more out of frustration or anger or she wants her way. I think she's pretty smart to know that if she throws a big enough fit, she might get what she wants. If she doesn't get what she wants, then she stops. Probably 90% of the time, she doesn't tantrum. But there are those rare occasions.

DAD: She gets mad like everybody else. She gets frustrated. Not very often. She's rarely, if ever, cried in her whole life.

MOM: Very seldom have I seen a true tear ... maybe once or twice. She is strong-willed. It's better than not caring. It makes it a little harder sometime, but I think in the end it will help her in life.

DAD: She doesn't have to worry about anything. We worry about her, but she's carefree. She's pretty much freelance. She does whatever she wants to do, whatever is going on that day.

MOM: She might act like she doesn't know what's going on, but she knows exactly what is going on around her.

DAD: She knows exactly. And she's really persnickety about her clothes. She only wears certain clothes and colors.

— RONNIE —

How is her communication?

MOM: You can give her direction. Her receptive language is pretty good. Most of the time, she can follow two or three step directions. She has language capability. She can say words. She mimics all of her CDs. She can mimic the words. It's not always clear to us, but she knows exactly what she's saying.

DAD: She'll carry on a conversation with her DVD. She memorizes them.

MOM: She even does the voice fluctuations almost perfectly. She has the language ability, but she doesn't use it for social communication. She'll say, "I want cookies," or "I want water." But she wouldn't tell you about what she did that day or how she's feeling or anything like that.

You wouldn't know she had an issue just by looking at her, unless you noticed that she doesn't interact, or until she starts making her noises. She doesn't sit and rock and flap and all that. She makes a loud noise when she gets excited, which can be annoying. We don't even notice it much anymore, because we hear it all the time.

What are her favorite things to do?

MOM: She loves Barney and Elmo. She sleeps with them every night: Barney, Elmo, Baby Bop and BJ, too. They are her best closest friends. They are who she has her conversations with. They are her favorites.

DAD: They're always covered up there on her bed, and she leaves the DVD player on for them when she's out here. Today, she brought out Barney, and she danced around with him.

MOM: She taught herself how to use the computer. We never showed her. We never showed her how to do a search or any of that.

DAD: When she first started using the computer, she would be watching a DVD on it, and she would turn the picture on the computer upside down and sideways. I don't know how she would do it. She just did it.

− RONNIE −

MOM: She has a red suitcase full of paper things. It's her prized possession. They're all books, or DVD covers, or the theater program from the Elmo Show, or papers with her characters on them. She'll take photographs out of the photo album and add them to her collection. We call it her "papers." When we go someplace, her sisters will bring their game players and their toys, and Ronnie brings her suitcase of papers. And with that, she's usually fine.

She's learning how to navigate the iPod. She wears headphones, and she listens to music. While she's at school she has music on pretty much the whole time. As long as she's working, and doing what she's supposed to be doing, she gets her music and she gets her papers at school. But if she stops, then they take away the papers and music.

A lot of our neighbors know Ronnie. It's helpful, because she has gotten out and gone across the street. If she's left a piece of paper at the neighbors, she'll go across the street and right into their house. We'll get a call, "Just wanted to let you know that Ronnie's here." The problem with her crossing the street is that she doesn't look. She's done it a few times. It's scary. So, we keep the door key way up high. She probably knows it's there. She's never attempted to get it and get out.

We don't go much of anywhere. It's only been in the last couple years that we've even gone to restaurants. When they were little, we used to go to Disneyland. Now she'll only tolerate it for maybe two hours. She wants to do what she wants to do. So, it's not much fun or worthwhile to go places. We travel in the motor home more than anything, because she's comfortable there.

DAD: When you say you have an autistic daughter, some people will ask you questions, to try to understand it, and some people just move away or change the subject. I just go where ever they go, because if they're not asking, I'm not giving them any information. That's my experience. If they ask me questions, I'm open to telling them whatever they want to know. But if they don't ask me any questions, we'll just move on to something else. Some people want to hear about it, some people don't.

— MADI —
10 YEARS | 1 MONTH

She has an amazing connection with animals, all animals. She's totally an animal whisperer. I remember when she was three or four she told me that she could talk "cat" and "dog."

Madi's mom

– MADI –

How would you describe Madi?

MOM: Madi definitely sees the world from a different point of view than the average person. She has an amazing connection with animals, all animals. She's totally an animal whisperer. I remember when she was three or four she told me that she could talk "cat" and "dog." She always seems to know what the dog wants. She's probably going to do something with animals when she gets older.

Before we even knew that Madi has Asperger's, the one thing in her life that made her focus was horses. From the time she was about three or four she was begging for horseback riding lessons. I searched everywhere for a trainer, and couldn't find one who would accept someone that young. Finally, I found someone who said that she could have lessons when she turned five. She's been riding with the same trainer since then.

Madi has always loved dogs too. My sister had a dog named Brandy who was very nervous and hyper. She was a stray that my sister had found. Brandy was so nervous that she would pee on everyone as you walked in the house. When Madi and I would go to visit, Brandy would immediately calm. Brandy would sit on the couch next to Madi. Madi could get Brandy into an almost trance like state just by petting her. Usually Brandy was going all day and never stopped for anyone until she passed out to sleep at night. But she would just put her head on Madi's lap and Madi would pet her and talk to her softly and Brandy would be in heaven.

Madi has always been able to do that with all animals. She has an affinity for all animals. I know that she'll be doing something with animals. She still has time to figure out what she wants to do. But it will definitely be with animals.

What else does Madi like to do?

MOM: She loves to read. She's an amazing reader. When she was in second grade we were supposed to keep a reading log. She was required by her teacher to read four hundred minutes a month. And every month she read over a thousand minutes. At the end of the year she got the award for being the most profuse reader in the second grade. No one had ever read that many hours. And that was when she first started to read.

– MADI –

Madi has always known what she likes and doesn't like. I signed her up for soccer camp when she was six or seven, because her best friend at the time was doing it. I had ordered shin guards for her. I'm in the process of paying for everything and she asked what the shin guards are for. I said, "They're to protect you so don't get kicked in the shins." She looked at me and said, "There is no way you are going to get me to play a game that gets you kicked in the shins," which is pretty smart. Thirty minutes of discussion later, I'm getting my refund.

In what areas is Madi still developing?

MOM: She doesn't do so well with sensory things. When she gets too hot or too cold, she's not very happy. And when she's not very happy she's a little bit more argumentative. I knew from the time she was a baby that there were sensory issues. The sensory issues were unbelievable. As a baby we couldn't get water on her face when we were washing her hair, or she would scream. She wouldn't wear shoes. Everything had to be cotton. There were sensory issues with food, especially texture issues. I always thought something was odd.

She's always been cautious. She had irrational fears. When she was two we had a birthday party and a balloon popped. From that point on we couldn't even eat at a restaurant that gave balloons to children. If we walked in and saw a balloon, we'd walk out, because otherwise it would have been solid screaming. And she has an amazing lung capacity. She'd be great in opera.

What is Madi's understanding of her diagnosis?

MOM: Madi was seven when she first got diagnosed. At the time her dad and I didn't think we really needed to say anything to her. But last spring when she was in third grade she started asking why it was so difficult for her on the playground. She'd come home from school and cry, saying that she had a hard day, because she didn't understand things that happened.

We had found a book about a boy with autism that was presented from his point of view. It talked about how he didn't like loud noises. He didn't like bright lights. He didn't like things that weren't soft cotton. He didn't like things that were too hot or too cold. He didn't like crowds. There was a list of all these things that he didn't like. She read this book and said. "That's me." At that point we decided that it was time to tell her. We took her to dinner and told her. And she said, "Well now it makes sense."

She's really brilliant in the way that she gets it. She understands concepts that a lot of kids her own age might not. One of the things that I keep telling her is that her ability to hyper-focus is going to be a gift when she gets a little older. Kids who have high-functioning autism, or Asperger's, which she has, are able to hyper-focus to the extent of tuning out everything else when they find their main interest in life. The average person is thinking about a lot of things at the same time. But the person who has Asperger's is only doing what they are doing. And that can be a gift later in life.

Madi had a sleep-over at a friend's house last night. Her friend's mom overheard them having a conversation about being on the autism spectrum and how it's a different way of thinking and how sometimes the neurons in your brain just don't connect the same way that they do with other people. It doesn't necessarily mean that there's something wrong with you. It just means that you're different.

— CHRISTIAN —
9 YEARS | 9 MONTHS

Jamey (older brother) and Christian

Normally he doesn't want to talk much during the day, but
sometimes when I'm trying to go to sleep, I'll hear this voice
coming from the top bunk, "Jamey, let's have a talk."

Jamey

– CHRISTIAN –

If someone heard that your son had autism, what would you want them to know about Christian?

MOM: I would want them to know that he is sensitive. He's not so completely detached from society. He understands when someone says something negative about him. He'll tell us if someone said something that hurt his feelings. Even if he is a little bit detached, he's still taking it all in.

DAD: Christian is a people person. Little kids love him. They'll run around and play with him. He makes friends very quickly with little kids. He likes to meet people. When we go to a restaurant he'll go to the next table and say "Hi. My name is Christian. What's your name?"

MOM: He'll pull up a chair and sit down with them. People will have this look on their face, like "Who is this child? Where are the parents?" As soon as we say, "I'm sorry. This is Christian. He has autism," they're usually accepting. He'll sit and have conversations with people. He'll eat ice cream with people. He'll eat dinner with people.

He's like a little ambassador for autism. And it sounds like you are open to sharing who he is.

DAD: So many times we have to because he looks normal and in some ways he acts normal, and then when he acts up people think he's a brat.

MOM: There have been times when people have said horrible things to us. There was one man that said, "If you can't control that animal, then don't leave the house with him" or a woman who came up to me and said, "There's not enough money in the world for that little brat to be my kid." We want to be kind and remember to be respectful, but at those times it's hard not to say, "We're sorry that you thought that we cared what your opinion was." People tend to be tolerant until it affects them. If it affects their quiet at dinner, or their peace and quiet at the grocery store, then they think they have license to tell you exactly what they think. And even more so with a special needs child. But, "No, I don't need your opinion … I'm fine thanks."

DAD: Sometimes we wish we could say, "Just spend a day in our shoes. You have no idea …" Most of the time when people give us the weird look, if we say "Oh, I'm sorry, he has autism," it's like a light goes on for them.

We have also seen some kindness. Christian has a seizure disorder and he was hooked up with electrodes for a twenty-four hour EEG. His head was all wrapped up in a turban. At a department store an older gentleman asked "Is he going to be O.K.?" It was this very kind precious moment. We said "Oh, he's just having tests done." He said, "Well, praise the Lord. Good luck to you." That was such a kind thing for him to do and it was the absolute opposite of being rude to you.

It was such a simple, beautiful sentiment and you still remember it years later.

MOM: Because we know Christian is an amazing guy. Christian is never trying to be mean or rude. He just says what's on his mind. We had an incident on the train a couple weeks ago. There was a very handsome, very well dressed gentleman on the train. You could tell he was a corporate man. And he was completely bald. Not a hair on his head. As he walked past us Christian said "Wow, that guy's really bald." The man turned to look at us, and I said, "I am so sorry." And he said, "It's O.K. He's right. I am bald." It was very sweet of him.

His older brother Jamey, who is eleven years old, has grown up very quickly. It's been amazing to see what he was able to get Christian to do that we couldn't, even at a young age,. We couldn't get him into pajamas. Jamey would say "Well come on Christian, don't you want to wear jammies like me?" It's so great that he has a big brother to emulate.

DAD: They share a room. Every night, Jamey and Christian will talk before they go to sleep. Once in a while Jamey will go away and you see how much Jamey does for Christian, or how much Christian depends on him. Christian and his little sister, Hailey, are more like partners, at least for the time being. They play together a lot. Cognitively they're on the same level in many ways. But Hailey, who is now six, is starting to pass up Christian. She's starting to read now, whereas Christian still has a lot of difficulty with reading.

MOM: And she's starting to know about autism. She'll ask "is that just for children with autism, or is it for all of us?" She's starting to differentiate. She's always known that he has issues. But she's getting more verbal about it and telling people about autism and about epilepsy.

When Jamey was about five years old, a little boy heard that Christian had epilepsy and asked what that was. And Jamey looked at him and said, "Oh, it's just a brain thing. You're eyes just go like this." It was the greatest five year old definition of epilepsy.

At a very young age, when a child would ask, "Why is your brother like that? Why is he weird?" Jamey would say, "He has autism." And if they asked, "What's that," he'd say, "It's just that your brain learns different." He's really good at telling people, "That's just the way my brother is." He also stands up for his brother when someone is mean. He takes Christian's side. He's a good protector.

So, Jamey, can I ask you a question? How would you describe autism?
JAMEY: I'd have to say it's basically that he may seem like a normal person on the outside, but on the inside he's actually kind of... his brain is making him do things that probably somebody else would not want to do. Since his brain is a little slower than ours he'll have to respond to his brain, of course, because it's the main part of the nervous system. That's basically what autism is. But just because he's autistic doesn't mean he's not a normal functioning person. It doesn't mean he can't play baseball or ride a bike like a regular person.

I hear that you guys have some pretty good conversations?
JAMEY: Yeah, we do. Normally he doesn't want to talk much during the day, but sometimes when I'm trying to go to sleep, I'll hear this voice coming from the top bunk, "Jamey, let's have a talk."

— MASON —

10 YEARS | 4 MONTHS

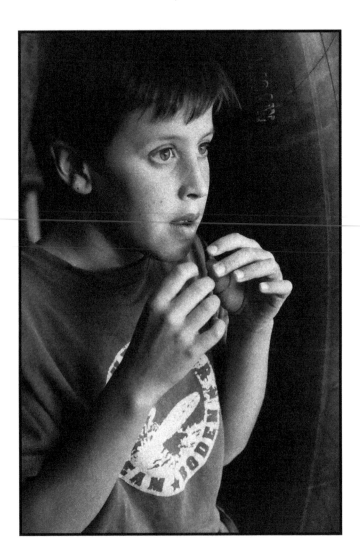

Mason is incredibly trusting. That's one of his greatest attributes, because it has got to be scary in his little world to just be following along and not really knowing what's going to happen next.

Mason's mom

You have two sons who are on the spectrum. How would you describe your younger son Mason?

MOM: Mason is more severely involved than Ian[19]. Kids stare, but it's understandable because with Mason it's more obvious. And his personality is sillier than Ian's. He definitely likes to have a good time. Mason is hard to read, particularly because he doesn't have much language. But his eyes are so telling. He has incredible eye contact. He's incredibly trusting. That's one of his greatest attributes, because it has got to be scary in his little world to just be following along and not really knowing what's going to happen next. He's been taken to the doctor to get blood drawn. He doesn't know what's going on and then it happens. He's really quite good about it.

DAD: He also has a good memory. We stayed at a motel on the beach and now every time we ride by it he wants to go in and watch his videos and jump on the bed. He loved that place.

MOM: Mason's favorite things to do are to play chase or play tickle. He also loves to swing. He loves watching videos. He loves going camping. He likes going places, like hotels, and swimming pools. He's a great swimmer. That's great, because some kids with autism have so much trouble with change that they can't even handle something like rearranging a piece of furniture in a room. He's pretty laid back in that way. We've always traveled and we've moved a lot. We've always tried to get out and do things. He also loves to be on a skateboard. He has great balance, though he still needs some help. He tried snowboarding with his dad. He's very trusting of his dad.

DAD: He's not blind to harm ...

MOM: ... but he does have poor safety awareness in some ways. He will run in the street with cars coming. When he does get hurt he has a high tolerance for pain. It's not a huge deal when he scrapes his knee.

DAD: Like a lot of autistic kids, his senses are super high. He can tell the difference between pizza brands by smelling them, to decide if it's the type he knows.

---

19   Ian, page 176

– MASON –

When was he diagnosed?

MOM: As a baby, he was growing typically. He was a little late in language. But then within about four months he was gone. He was about eighteen months old or so. We took him in for testing at twenty months old and they said "No, he's ok." He had started laughing to himself while looking out into space, which is what his brother Ian used to do. We just thought, "Oh, no." We took him back for testing right after his second birthday and it was very clear.

DAD: He had hit a dark zone. He wouldn't communicate at all. He went to the dark side real fast. He looked almost sick. It was pretty dramatic.

MOM: It was very sad. I don't know what happened. He's more severe than his older brother Ian, who is also on the spectrum. Mason has a lot of sensory problems.

DAD: If there are too many people talking or too much going on, he'll blow a fuse. He gets really bothered by Ian's talking.

MOM: Ian has a real issue with Mason. Mason screams and Ian doesn't like that. They definitely push each other's buttons.

DAD: Half the time Mason has his fingers in his ears.

MOM: And it's not always because of noise. Sometimes it's just because it's become a habit.

DAD: He does it mostly when he's out his comfort zone. He does pretty well at home. And he doesn't do it when we're camping, which is one of his favorite things. When he's in unfamiliar places or around unfamiliar people he has his fingers in his ears. When we're out in the community, most people are decent. Autism is becoming so common. But, every once in a while you'll have someone who is just nasty.

MOM: Mason will scream very loud, just out of the blue. It scares me when he does it in the car. It's all peaceful, we're listening to music, and then all of a sudden he'll scream. The biggest nightmare is when he screams in an airport or on an airplane. We were going through security and some nasty lady commented. He looks so typical that they think he's being a brat when he's screaming. We get a few of those, but more often we get stares. Mostly it looks like they are trying to figure out what's wrong. It is pretty obvious, after a while, that he's got something. I just avoid the grocery store or any place that will be difficult for him. But sometimes even in places that he likes he'll have a melt-down. We were riding bikes down by the beach and he got upset when we turned around to go back.

DAD: He might have thought that we were going somewhere in particular and got upset when we made a U-turn. He had a meltdown.

Is he able to communicate with his family?

MOM: Mason's biggest challenge is his lack of speech. But he communicates fairly well around here, which is huge. We understand him. He probably has too many things done for him. He could probably do more on his own. But we just want him to be comfortable and happy, and not upset and screaming. He can have quite a temper. Sometimes he gets very frustrated. You want to keep your house sane in some ways and if you push too hard it will just completely crumble.

DAD: Sometimes he seems very present and very typical. He knows exactly what he wants and he doesn't seem confused about it. Everything else is the actions that his body makes him do and he can't help it. Sometimes he has perfect focus on what he wants. But then other times, maybe not. Distractions are too much for him and he can't always control his body movements. I've seen that. There are times when it looks like there's a lot going on in his head.

MOM: Definitely. Then suddenly he has to run across the room, or he has to climb under his blankets.

DAD: If there was a book about Mason it would probably be called "I Am in Here."

— ELEVEN TO THIRTEEN YEARS —

Once you get past the original diagnosis, you start seeing your child develop and you watch their personality develop. Each has a very specific personality, which a lot of people don't realize or understand. And then, as they start to get older, you think, "Oh, it's not what I thought it was going to be." You're still working through the diagnosis and trying to come to terms with everything, but it's actually a lot more positive than you were initially given to understand.

– *Isabella's mom*

Sometimes parents get in a rut. You think you know your child and you're so used to doing certain things for them that you automatically brush their hair or brush their teeth or choose their clothes. You have to give them a chance. Maybe they can do more, as they mature and as they receive therapy. Maybe she wants a ponytail one day or her hair down on another. You have to retrain yourself to ask her how she wants her hair done.

– *Parisa's mom*

Sometimes I look back at the more difficult years and think "how did we do it?" I realized that we took our job seriously as parents. You do the best that you can for your child. And you let people know when you need help. Pride is not a good thing when you're trying to raise a child with a disability. You just have to hunker down and take it all in and realize that it's going to be okay.

– *Eleni's mom*

— LUCAS —
11 YEARS | 1 MONTH

Lucas is very sweet and wants to trust everybody. If people are nice
to him he thinks they're his friend. He doesn't realize that people
can have bad intentions.

Lucas' mom

– LUCAS –

How would you describe Lucas?

MOM: Lucas is a good person. That's just a fact. He's a happy kid. He's in a good spot. He's very well adjusted. He's got a good temperament. His biggest challenge is his ADD issues, as far as focusing and staying on task. There are some learning disabilities, but he's doing well. Lucas loves his school. He's outgoing and social. He loves talking to people. He loves little kids. He's always been into music. He's into cell phones and telephones, so that may be an avenue he's able to pursue later in life.

I am trying to teach him to advocate for himself if he has an issue, a problem to solve, to figure out how he's going to work it out. He has seen me do this for him his whole life. He and his best friend at school recently set up a meeting with their principal, because they were having some issues with some of the kids. I had heard them complaining about these kids from school. I said, "You guys have been talking about this for a long time. Why don't you set up a meeting with your teacher and the principal?" They thought that was a great idea.

A couple weeks later, I heard Lucas talking on the phone with his friend about what they were going to wear for their big meeting with the principal. They were talking about dressing up and wearing ties. So I emailed the principal and said, "FYI, just so you know, the boys think they have a meeting with you tomorrow." I would have loved to have been a fly on the wall. The principal emailed me back the next day and told me that they had met, the boys had told her what their issues were and they discussed different problem solving ideas. It was great.

Lucas and his best friend talk on the phone all the time. His friend's mom once said, "We spent all this time and money chauffeuring the kids back and forth to speech therapy and social skills classes and all it took was cell phones." That's how they connected.

In some ways he's very easy going, but then there are also the meltdowns and some occasional rigidness. Lucas loves to plan. He's pretty easy about going to speech or OT. But if he knows that we're planning to go, for instance, to Grandma's this weekend and then we have to reschedule it, he has a meltdown. We try to prevent this from happening by not telling him about it until we know for sure. If we know someone is coming to visit, like the cousins from Connecticut, we wait until the last possible minute to tell him. Otherwise the excitement and the anxiety leading up to it is too much.

That's good for new parents to know. What are other adaptations that you've made over time?

MOM: My biggest suggestion to other parents would be pre-plan, pre-plan, pre-plan. When he was little we were constantly making little story boards. His aunt got married when he was about four. We had to have people that he'd never met come to baby-sit him. So, I sent them a disposable camera and asked them to please take some pictures of themselves. I sent them a prepaid envelope to send it back in. I printed up large prints and told him, "These are the people who are going to be taking care of you." If he had a new teacher coming up, I'd take her picture beforehand, so he would know what she looked like.

They had a Halloween parade every year at the school where he was going to be attending kindergarten. It always took place on the day before Halloween. While he was still in preschool, I decided to tape the Halloween parade at the kindergarten that he would be attending the following year. When he was actually in the kindergarten, for the whole week before Halloween, we watched the tape so he would see what was going to happen at the Halloween parade the next day.

We don't need to plan ahead so much with him anymore. Now he makes his own plans. Sometimes, he'll make lists for himself. He was at his Grandma's last week for Spring Break. Before he went, he planned out what they would do every day and then he called his grandparents and told them. He's into planning. He wants to know what's going to happen.

– LUCAS –

How does he do when you're out in the community?

MOM: Now he does really well out in public. But when he was about three or four, we were at the customer service counter at a department store and he was out of control. We didn't have the diagnosis yet. I remember this snobby, older woman saying, "Well if that was my child he would not be acting that way." And I said, "Well, then thank God he's not your child."

I have had other people say things to me, but in the last couple years I've had no problem saying, "Listen, I appreciate your concern, but just so you know my son has autism." People have more understanding now about autism, or at least they have heard of it, because of where we are now as a society, and because of Hollywood. If needed, I have no issue saying my son has a diagnosis of autism.

In the fourth grade, when Lucas was still in the public school, we were having serious issues with bullying. He is so naïve that he became an easy target for the bullies. Lucas is very sweet and wants to trust everybody. If people are nice to him he thinks they're his friend. He doesn't realize that people can have bad intentions. It wasn't the right place for him at that time

He's in fifth grade now and the private school he's attending is for kids with autism. They're good about taking away the anxiety around social issues. The kids there are much more comfortable and so they're able to blossom.

When you're dealing with autism, every day is a success. A day without meltdowns, that's a success. Since we've been at this new school, there have been very few meltdowns. He has less anxiety and stress. He's in a good place.

— ISABELLA —

11 YEARS | 2 MONTHS

Isabella has a particular quirky little personality. She has a very humorous side to her. She likes to wind people up. She will say things that she knows are wrong and then look at you to see what your reaction is going to be.

Isabella's mom

– ISABELLA –

What would you like to tell me about Isabella?

MOM: Once you get past the original diagnosis, you start seeing your child develop and you watch their personality develop. Each has a very specific personality, which a lot of people don't realize or understand. And then, as they start to get older, you think, "Oh, it's not what I thought it was going to be." You're still working through the diagnosis and trying to come to terms with everything, but it's actually a lot more positive than you were initially given to understand.

How would you describe her personality?

MOM: Isabella has a particular quirky little personality. She has a very humorous side to her. She likes to wind people up. She will say things that she knows are wrong and then look at you to see what your reaction is going to be. She knows it's going to make people laugh. It's quite fun to watch her as she's developing. She's so funny.

Isabella is very warm and loving. I think most people have a misconception that you won't get the warmth that you get with a typical child. That's wrong. She gives the biggest hugs. She gets very excited when you return from somewhere. She'll come running down the stairs and tell you that she's missed you. In lots of ways she's easier because she doesn't argue with you as much as typical kids would, though I think we're heading in that direction. She's getting a little more determined than she used to be. She can be grumpy and we're getting some definite attitude as she's getting older.

She's very detailed oriented with her art work. She could be a graphic artist or something along those lines. She does the most beautiful drawings. What amazes me is that she draws from memory. She may go through a phase of doing the same picture over and over. It depends on what she's into at the time. But it's the bright, bold colors that she uses. For most of her birthdays she'll get markers and new sketch books because she goes through them like they're going out of style. Even when she was still in preschool, she would stay inside the lines when she drew a picture and the colors would always be bright and vibrant. I love it that everything is so bold and colorful.

– ISABELLA –

How is she with her peers?

MOM: She has quite a few friends. I think her friends have become a lot more open because of knowing Isabella. They enjoy her and get a kick out of her sense of humor. She gives them big hugs. She loves playing chase with them on the playground. I think they understand that even though she can't do everything that they are doing, they can still have a great friendship with somebody who might not fit into their typical age group friendship. They have a lot of fun together.

Isabella's younger brother adores her. They're very cute together and they're both very funny. We don't have to deal with the whole sibling rivalry thing. They'll sit in bed at night and read stories. She has certain books that she likes. She's very good at doing all the voices and all the intonations. At school they actually had Isabella go into the kindergarten class and read a story to the kindergarteners, because she's such a great story teller. Her aide said the kids were just mesmerized. They all sat quietly. They loved it. She is not shy in any way, shape, or form.

In what areas is she still developing?

MOM: The biggest area she's still developing is social engagement. She is showing more interest in being socially engaged with people in general, though it's still a difficult area for her. Academically, she's behind, but she's progressing. She's in a typical classroom and goes to the learning center for extra help. We recently did some testing with her and found that her basic foundational skills, like word attack, site reading, and spelling, are all at or above grade level. She has to work on comprehending what she's reading and then being able to use it.

She is very picky about what she'll eat, though it's getting a little better. She's a bit more willing to try some different things. But she won't go near fruits or vegetables. Her brother is a big fruit eater and she won't sit near him when he's eating it. Or she'll cover her mouth with her hands. She can't stand it. But she's getting a little better. She'll eat a little more meat than she used to. So we're sort of leaning a little bit that way. She definitely likes pasta, french fries, and all the good starchy food. Thankfully, she's very active. She's very bouncy.

She takes a while to get to sleep, but when she's asleep, she stays asleep. When she was younger, we went through a phase where she'd wake up about 3:00 in the morning, and then that was it. She'd be awake for the rest of the night. But it wasn't too bad.

Is she comfortable out in the community?

MOM: Isabella was never difficult out in public. She's never been a child for having tantrums or melt downs. So in that respect she's always been very easy. She is very nervous flying. The last time we went on a plane she kept putting the window screen up and down, up and down, up and down. Eventually, I did turn to the people behind us and said "I do apologize, but she's very nervous. She'll settle down in a bit." And she did. Mostly she's very easy. She certainly has some quirky behaviors, though often people who don't know her will be surprised when they hear that she has autism.

Isabella has made such a huge difference to my life in a positive way. She's made me stronger and more confident than I used to be. And I've become more tolerant of things that would have bothered me in the past. Now it's more like "It's O.K. It's fine. It's really not that important."

— MATTHEW —

11 YEARS | 6 MONTHS

I want people to know that Asperger's is just a different way of thinking.
And that under this stubborn rock-hard core I have a bright mind just
waiting to be uncovered... You have to dig hard for it.

Matthew

— MATTHEW —

What would you like people to know about you, Matt?

MATT: I want people to know that Asperger's is just a different way of thinking. And that under this stubborn rock-hard core I have a bright mind just waiting to be uncovered. It's like, there's a diamond hidden by a thick wall of rock. I'm this bright, intelligent gem buried under five hundred tons of rock. You have to dig hard for it.

MOM: That's a challenge that you face. How can you get somebody who has so much inside to be able to put it out there so that the rest of the world can see it? And, the rest of the world doesn't always get that you're so sensitive. What are other challenges for you?

MATT: Fighting against my temper; and what other people think of me. Some people who don't know me well might think that I'm just a stubborn and stupid kid who to the slightest aggravation starts screaming and running around.

We have weight equipment upstairs and the pressure helps me get my stress out when I'm really frustrated. It helps me from going on a little wild rampage. And I like being in the pool because I feel so relaxed. It's like every single stress is banished from my mind.

You said that you used to get really bugged by slimy stuff on your hands. How did it make you feel?

MATT: It made me feel, "Ewww. Get off me. Get it off me. Get it off me!" It feels very unwelcome. It feels like I have a hot coal in the palm of my hand.

Does it feel like something you want to get out of your hand quickly?

MATT: Yes!

MOM: What about noise?

MATT: Noise can be the largest problem. I really crank up and go overload. It feels like "Arrgh!" Like I can't take it.

MOM: Does your mind shut down?

MATT: More like self-destruct.

MOM: And you also hear things better than most people. In some ways it's sort of like a super power. And in some ways it gets in the way.

MATT: It's like your greatest strength is your greatest weakness.

So, what do you do in those situations?

MATT: Oh, I usually try to get to a quieter location if I can. And sometimes I just contribute to the noise by screaming and running around.

Do you have a favorite story about Matt?

MOM: There was when he learned how to ride a bike. His occupational therapist taught him. We had all tried to teach him. But she was the one that did it. And he was nine. Everybody knows how to ride their bike before then. Soon after he learned to ride a bike we went to Yosemite. We were all able to bike around the valley together. I called Matt's OT and told her, "You made our vacation. I don't think you understand how fundamentally you affected our lives." It was the culmination of everything she had done that changed the quality of our life. That bike ride was so symbolic. My husband cried. I cried. Everybody cried. It was a really wonderful thing. The OT later said that she wished she could frame that voice mail message. She said it was the best message she had ever received. I sent her pictures of him on the bike. It really was a big success. People who have autistic kids understand what that means. You really do change your vision. You change how you see things.

What are some things that Matt does really well?

MOM: Matthew is very perceptive and insightful. Another favorite story just happened. He had an assignment for school to choose a poem, analyze it and write a paragraph about it to be presented to the class. Matt is an animal expert, among other expertise, so he picked the poem "The Tiger" by William Blake.

One of the questions on the assignment was, "Who do you think this was for? Why did the poet write it?" When I asked Matt he looked at me and said, "Well, looking at the dates of his birth and death, he lived during the age of enlightenment. At this point in time they were studying science and getting into things like whether or not God really exists. So wouldn't somebody who created this fierce and vicious creature have to be a God?" And, I'm sitting there thinking, "Okay, that is what it says. But I didn't know that until college."

What he said was a beautiful thing because it put together so much. It shows just how much is going on in his head. It doesn't necessarily come out in his writing, but it does come out verbally. You have to be creative. You have to be able to access him in a different way. That's the challenge that you face. How can you get somebody who's got so much inside be able to bring it out so that the rest of the world can see it?

Is there anything you'd like to say to other parents of kids with ASD?

MOM: When I had twins, even before Matt's autism diagnosis, the doctor said, "You need help. You don't know you need help, but you need help. And people will want to help. Give them things to do. When they ask, you can't just say, 'I don't know'. You say, 'When you go to the store, could you please pick up eggs and milk for me' or 'Do you mind coming over and just sitting in their room while I take a shower? You have to be very specific." It's the same thing when you have a child with autism who is having a melt-down. I would want other parents to know that there are people who are very kind.

Most people just don't know what to do. The more direction you can give people the better. I would say, "I need a quiet place for him," or "I have to take him outside. Can you watch my other son?" It helps if you can give specific directions. People will respond. They really do.

— AMBERLY —

12 YEARS | 9 MONTHS

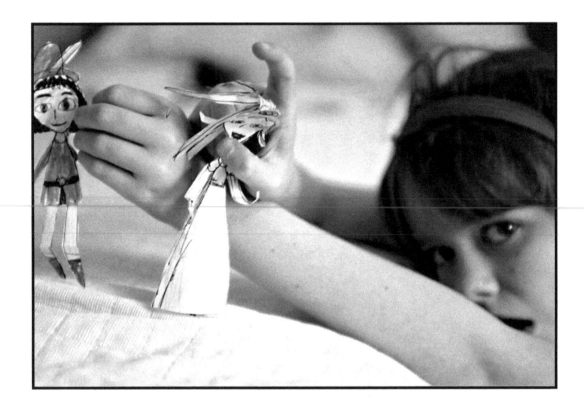

Amberly is very artistic. She loves to draw. She made a picture of some
exercise girls from a video... She drew them with the correct perspective,
with the people in the back smaller than those in front. It looks realistic.

Amberly's mom

− AMBERLY −

People sometimes make assumptions about autism. If someone knew that Amberly has autism but hadn't met her yet what would you like them to know about her?

MOM: Amberly is very interested in meeting people, which isn't always typical of others with autism. She's very social. She and her sister Brittany[20] love little kids and like to talk to them. Amberly will go up to little kids at the OT clinic and say, "Hi," while bending down and shaking their hand. She'll say, "How are you? I'm Amberly." She enjoys talking and making contact, even with people she doesn't know.

Our church has social events, and Amberly will talk some to people there. Last week, a little boy was crying. Amberly went over to him, patted him on the head and said, "You're okay. It's alright. Don't cry. Don't cry." Amberly sometimes talks to one of the girls that is in her group at church. They socialize on more of a superficial level. They can't maintain it. They'll say, "Hi. How are you? I like you." And, then, they'll move on. Amberly mostly likes to skip and dance in the open space.

Amberly is very affectionate, kind and thoughtful most of the time. She's very energetic and spunky. She used to worry us because she had no safety awareness. She was on the go all the time. She is much better, with lot of practice at school and in therapy. Amberly is very artistic. She loves to draw. She made a picture of some exercise girls from a video that we have. She drew them lined up in a V formation. She drew them with the correct perspective, with the people in the back smaller than those in front. It looks realistic.

She is happy most of the time, although she is a little more moody as she is becoming a teenager. When she was younger, she would throw tantrums because she couldn't be understood and would get frustrated. Now that her language has improved, her tantrums have diminished quite a bit. When she's mad she will run upstairs to her bedroom and slam the door. It's very typical teenage behavior. If I come in the room, she'll go into her closet. Then I know for sure that she has to have some down time. Mostly, she's pretty good. She gets over things pretty quickly. She doesn't internalize much.

---

20   Brittany, page 206

Amberly also loves to dance. We put on music and she just dances. I used to teach dance classes, but she doesn't really take instruction. She likes free style, which is actually kind of nice. We also have an exercise video that she likes. She gets her physical activity in through dance and exercise.

Amberly could sing before she could talk. To help her develop her language we would speak in a sing-song way. She would pay attention to it more. We would also sometimes pretend that we didn't know what she wanted. She might indicate that she wanted juice by pulling us or pointing to it. But I'd purposely get her water instead, which she hated. I'd hand her a glass of water and say, "Here's your drink." She'd get so mad. Finally, one day she shoved the water away and said, "Juice."

One of the boys in Amberly's preschool class always looked out for her. He made sure no one bothered her. One day I went to visit the class, as I did from time to time. He came running up to me and said, "She can talk! She can talk!" Up until then she hadn't been verbal at school.

Amberly's speech still isn't 100% clear, but she has speech. She can put together small sentences and, once in a while, longer sentences. She has on days and off days. Some days, she doesn't talk much. Other days, she talks a lot.

How is she with sleep?

MOM: Amberly is much better with sleep than she used to be. Her biggest problem was getting to sleep. She would take a long time, sometimes hours, to get to sleep. Then she'd have a hard time getting up in the morning. Amberly liked the movie, "Annie" and she would have to physically act out the entire movie before she could go to bed. She wouldn't go to bed until 1:00 or 2:00 in the morning. She'd still be singing, "Tomorrow, tomorrow." She'd throw a sheet or blanket over a chair, because in the movie the kids were hiding the dog. And, she'd sit in the windowsill and sing like Annie. She was only about four years old. She couldn't really sing the words. She couldn't really even talk yet. I was exhausted because I never got much sleep.

How does she feel about school?

MOM: Amberly loves school and most of the time she does well. She loves the routine. Occasionally she will fake being sick if she doesn't want to do something. Amberly just finished sixth grade, so next year she'll be in middle school. She doesn't seem to be too worried. She's been over to the new school a few times. Amberly is better at math than reading. She understands the math concepts. She can do subtraction and addition with three digits, and knows how to borrow and carry over. She's not as good at reading and doesn't care much for it. That's mostly when she fakes being sick. Reading and writing are really stressful for her.

And what about friends?

MOM: Amberly has friends from her special education class at school. They hang out together on the playground. They'll hook arms and skip across the field. They'll swing and play on the slide. They're happy. The typical kids in the school also talk to Amberly. A good thing about her school is that they have inclusion. Otherwise, she could be excluded so much. She's in a regular education homeroom for about twenty minutes at a time. She likes it, and the kids seem to like her. When we get to the school, I'll hear, "Hi, Amberly" a lot.

Amberly has improved a lot over the past few years. She's not running off or biting any more. She really enjoys people. She's socially awkward, but she makes an attempt. Amberly is very energetic and was more tomboyish than her sister. She liked playing rough. Now, because of her sister's influence, she likes princesses and more girly things. She's developed a lot of personality. And she's happy most of the time.

— ELENI —

13 YEARS | 7 MONTHS

Eleni and her younger sister Kate

Eleni has a very loving spirit and she will do anything for her younger sister, Kate... They play games that they have made up together. It's a way for Kate to bring Eleni in and try to get her to interact in different ways.

Eleni's dad

What would you like people to know about your daughter?

MOM: That Eleni is a beautiful child inside and out. She's a gift. She's got this unique ability to reach into the hearts of people and find their soft spot.

DAD: She's a happy kid and she enjoys laughing.

MOM: She makes an impression on everyone she meets.

DAD: Although people's response to her can be mixed. People who know her, and aren't intimidated, enjoy her and try to interact with her. People who don't know anything about autism are often leery and nervous around her in the beginning. It's something different and they don't know how to handle it. I'd like people to know that they don't have to be afraid. She's trying the best she can and she's a good person. Her best characteristic is that she has this impish sense of humor.

MOM: And she has a great smile that lights her up from the inside out. It's contagious. When she gets that little impish, flirty quality about her, people just melt. They get entranced under her spell.

DAD: Eleni has a very loving spirit and she will do anything for her younger sister, Kate. They don't have a typical sister relationship, because most sisters fight some of the time. But these two get along really well. Whatever Kate wants, Eleni gives her. And Kate does everything for Eleni. For most of her life, Kate has taken on a therapist role for Eleni. They play games that they have made up together. It's a way for Kate to bring Eleni in and try to get her to interact in different ways.

MOM: Kate has become the "older" sister.

For the parents of children on the spectrum there are so many different therapies and approaches to choose from. How did you make the choices you made?

MOM: At the time that Eleni was diagnosed all these "best practice" approaches were starting to come out. For many of them we didn't see enough significant data to warrant changing around Eleni's life. Some of the approaches just seemed like someone got published and then got on the map. We preferred to stay with science. With my background in speech and linguistics, I knew that research was important. I didn't really understand much about sensory integration partly because I have sensory sensitivities myself that I had always just lived with. What I read about occupational therapy using sensory integration just made sense. The approach also follows the child's lead, building on their ideas. That's always been the best way with Eleni. She has to buy into the program in order for the program to work. Eleni has always had an independent spirit, even when she was nonverbal. She would definitely make her wants known. She didn't tantrum, but she's a bit headstrong. I've always respected her individuality.

What are Eleni's interests, strengths, and talents?

DAD: One of Eleni's main interests is music. She likes all kinds of music. And she loves watching videos, until she has all the script down and knows the inflections of all the characters.

MOM: She is also definitely a visual learner. She has almost a photographic memory. When she was about five years old we went out to a restaurant, which was a big deal for us. We chose to go for an early dinner, when we thought it would be quiet, so she wouldn't go ballistic with all the noise. We sit down at the booth, get the crayons out, get ready to color, and I know that this is going to be a fabulous meal. Then in comes a huge birthday party and they sit down very near to us. Should we leave? We've already placed our order. What are we going to do? Eleni started getting a little fidgety with the sound. So I turned the placemat over and I wrote "Eleni is in the restaurant." And she read "Eleni is in the restaurant." My husband looked at me, I looked at him. We were shocked. She had just read. I hadn't said it out loud. I had only written it.

I wrote, "Eleni is a girl." And she said "Eleni is a girl." Then she stared at the paper, waiting for me to write the next words. So I started writing "Eleni is okay," "It's noisy," "We are going to be okay," "We're going to eat dinner and then we're going to go home." And she calmed down. That's when we realized that she could read. That was really her first form of communication. She didn't understand everything she was reading but she could read words. She knew the letters. Her actual language just kind of evolved from that. Now she's in sixth grade and can read the sixth grade books, but her comprehension is at a second grade level. She doesn't necessarily understand the context and all the social nuances.

DAD: We're working on her comprehension.

MOM: During her "Daddy time" they read the newspaper comics pages together. Eleni assigns the roles. She'll say "I'm the Blondie and you be Dagwood."

DAD: And if Dagwood doesn't have a lot to say, then she's fine doing the whole thing. It's something for us to do together

MOM: We're doing a lot to keep her in an inclusive environment. You have to fight and advocate for your child constantly. She has her sensory issues and it takes a lot for her to maintain her status quo and a sense of normalcy for forty five minutes in each of her various classes. She's not always focused on the lecture. We modify curriculum. Her aide is taking notes and helping her.

When I became a mom I signed on for whatever could happen. And fortunately and unfortunately "whatever" did happen to us. We've been challenged through the years. Sometimes I look back at the more difficult years and think "how did we do it?" I realized that we took our job seriously as parents. You do the best that you can for your child. And you let people know when you need help. Pride is not a good thing when you're trying to raise a child with a disability. You just have to hunker down and take it all in and realize that it's going to be okay. It might seem like a death sentence, but it is really more of a life altering sentence. And you choose how you want to alter your life. It's a personal choice.

— IAN —
13 YEARS | 2 MONTHS

Ian is pretty agile. He is courageous... He's gotten up on a surfboard, but he prefers the boogie board. He likes the action. He's an adrenaline junkie.

Ian's dad

How would you describe Ian's personality?

DAD: Ian can be sensitive, and he can be very loving. He has that advantage over some kids with autism, who aren't as aware and emotionally tuned in as he is. He loves action and he has a lot of faith in his abilities.

MOM: He has a huge personality. He'll take risks. It's helped him to discover himself and do as well as he has. He's amazing at video games. He picks them up very quickly. His eye-hand coordination is great. He loves skateboarding, snowboarding and activities like that.

DAD: Ian is pretty agile. He is courageous. When I take him out surfing, if he gets pummeled under the water, he's not frightened. He does really well. He's gotten up on a surfboard, but he prefers the boogie board. He likes the action. He's an adrenaline junkie.

Ian also has a great memory. He'll notice if you have a new haircut, or if you're wearing new shoes. He tends to repeat questions many times. It's the only way he knows to get involved in a conversation. Sometimes he does it just to be there and interact. He doesn't know what else to say, so he starts asking questions that he already knows the answers to. He might like that we're telling him something he's familiar with and that's what he wants to hear. It might be his way of thinking out loud. Maybe it's what is in his head and he has to bring it out into words

When he was asking me questions he seemed to be as interested in watching my expressions as he was in listening to my response.

MOM: At least seventy-five percent of the time he knows the answers to his questions. But he likes to hear them over and over again. However, the constant questions can be incredibly tiring. Sometimes I'll say, "You just asked that question. Why are you asking it again?" And he'll say, "I have to." It is kind of an obsessive-compulsive type of thing, as well. But for the most part, for what he has to deal with, he does really well.

DAD: Ian is very fashion aware. He definitely cares about how he looks.

MOM: He's done the whole black Goth thing. He likes tattoos. It will be a little scary when he turns eighteen, and can make his own choices.

He looks like a rock star in the recent school photo you showed me. He has the stance, all the coolness, and that crooked smile.

DAD: He has always been very likeable. A lot of guys his age like his boldness.

MOM: Adults usually like his honesty, although kids sometimes have a hard time with him. Our middle son is eleven years old and typical. When he has his friends over, it takes them a little time to get adjusted to Ian's honesty. He'll ask very blunt questions. The kids can be a little bit taken back by that. You have to look past all of the quirkiness to understand him, which is sometimes hard for kids to do.

But for the most part they've all been pretty receptive to him. And Ian is becoming more socially aware. He sees his brother with his friends and he's realizing what is typical.

DAD: He likes to watch them. He likes to see what people are doing. If somebody is boring, not doing much of anything, he's not as interested in them. He likes to see kids doing goofy things. He likes to be entertained by other children. But he is also very private. He loves to have his own space. It is very important to him. He closes his door and no one can go in. He likes privacy.

Is he very social at school?

MOM: We would like to see him have more opportunities to interact with typical kids at school. He has the potential in him. There are a lot of the kids in his class that aren't that involved. He does have one friend that is quite autistic. Ian really likes him. But it is not a typical situation and I'd really like to see more of that for Ian. I'm trying to find other social situations for him outside of school. He gets along well with his cousins. They care about him and treat him nicely and typically. He likes that.

– IAN –

Ian is in a hard place. He knows that he is autistic. His youngest brother, Mason[21], has the same autistic label, but is much more involved, so Ian doesn't see himself as being like him. Ian sees his younger typical brother hanging out with his friends, and Ian can get a bit angry and jealous. His brother doesn't boast or anything about who he is and he would love to be able to hang out with Ian. But, Ian can be difficult. He will scream at him, "I hate you," and then the next minute Ian is nice and wants to play video games with him. It's sad because Ian could be a good friend to our middle son.

DAD: It's important for people to not take it too personally when he says overly blunt things. Sometimes we'll have people over and he'll say, "Why are they here?"

MOM: ... or "I don't want them to be here, I want it to be just our family," that type of thing.

DAD: It's not that he doesn't like them. He does that to everybody. He's pretty much an open book.

MOM: This past year has been really good for him, even though he complains about school all the time. It's been a turning point. He has become more social and more flexible. He's more able to let people enter his world. In the past he would be more closed off. He's managing very well considering his issues.

---

21   Mason, page 150

— PARISA —

13 YEARS | 6 MONTHS

Shayna (older sister) and Parisa

While Parisa doesn't have some of the skills that other children have, she also doesn't have some of the "negatives." She would never want to hurt anyone. She's never jealous... There's a purity in her emotional and mental makeup that is different from most other children.

Parisa's dad

Shayna, how would you describe your sister's personality?

SHAYNA: Parisa is very sweet and innocent. She's happy all the time and she's very enthusiastic. She's more motivated than I am about a lot of things. She's also very affectionate. Sometimes in the morning when she's supposed to be coming in to wake me up, instead she'll lie down next to me on the bed. She likes hugs and kisses, which is O.K. with family, but she needs to learn certain boundaries with other people. It is nice that she likes to be around people. That's a good thing.

DAD: Shayna is really great with Parisa. She is an expert on everything Parisa, even more than we are. In fact, sometimes Shayna will point out something with Pari that we missed.

MOM: Parisa is a great kid. We couldn't ask for a better. She's very curious. She loves cooking. She has a lot of fun being with other kids. She loves going to school. She takes pride in what she does. She always wants to do her best, which in a way is also a weakness because she's a bit of a perfectionist. She gets upset if she makes a mistake. She tries so hard to do what you want her to do. She does best if you demonstrate while you're explaining it to her.

DAD: Sometimes she'll repeat back to you things that you say. It's her way of letting us know that she knows what she's supposed to do. Her receptive language is much higher than her expressive language.

Does her difficulty with expressive language affect her ability to socialize?

MOM: For Parisa, the hardest thing about interacting with people is her language. She'll get frustrated because she wants to tell us something and we don't understand. She's come a long way, but there are still times when it's hard to understand her. The most frustrating times are when she starts crying and we don't know if she is hurting or if she's sad or what is wrong.

In elementary school they had "student of the week" awards. The teachers would let Parisa be one of the first kids to receive it. We would use her presentation as an opportunity for disability awareness.

– PARISA –

We would show pictures of Parisa rock climbing, kayaking and ice skating. The kids would realize that she could do some things they couldn't do. We would explain, "Parisa really likes to do things with you guys but sometimes she's not able to express herself. You can help her learn things." Then all of a sudden they would be Parisa's buddy. Many of the kids really enjoyed helping her learn to do things. Even the boys would teach her how to shoot hoops and things like that. They were so patient. The kids were sometimes more open-minded than the teachers.

DAD: She likes to be around other people. She doesn't shy away when we have friends over to the house. She likes listening to the conversations and being part of it all. In noisy places she'll sometimes put her hands over her ears, but she also likes a certain amount of stimulation in places where there are a lot of people. That's another way that she's different from the stereotypes of autism.

MOM: She picks up gross motor activities really quickly and likes lots of outdoor activities. If we keep her busy, she actually focuses better. She also loves music. It can be frustrating because sometimes she can't do very basic things, while other times she'll do things that are at a higher level and involve more cognitive skills.

DAD: She goes bowling and rollerblading with her sister, and has attended some hip hop dance classes. She participated in an after-school basketball program, and gymnastics classes. She's really willing to try just about anything. It took a long time for her to learn to ride a bicycle, especially the concept of steering. We had almost given up and then she just got it. We have to remind ourselves that with some things we have to keep trying for a long time. We'll get close to giving up and then suddenly she gets it. One thing that is difficult for her is to initiate play activities on her own. If you don't give her a suggestion, she'll sit on the couch for a long time and just twirl objects. The computer is a big motivator for her.

– PARISA –

MOM: Parisa has changed a lot over time. Over the last year she stopped flapping her arms. We don't know what happened. All of the sudden, she stopped.

Sometimes parents get in a rut. You think you know your child and you're so used to doing certain things for them that you automatically brush their hair or brush their teeth or choose their clothes. You have to give them a chance. Maybe they can do more, as they mature and as they receive therapy. Maybe she wants a ponytail one day or her hair down on another. You have to retrain yourself to ask her how she wants her hair done.

Now, at the mall, she chooses her own clothes. She notices what the other kids are wearing. She gravitates towards clothes that are cool and that she sees on other kids. Now, she dresses just like typical kids. It helps others to associate more easily with her. She gets this sense of pride from choosing her own clothes. She's much happier because she can make more of her own choices now. She can choose what color she wants to wear, or where she wants to sit, or what she's going to eat. That's what life is all about. We want our kids to be able to make choices that affect the quality of their life.

DAD: While Parisa doesn't have some of the skills that other children have, she also doesn't have some of the "negatives." She would never want to hurt anyone. She's never jealous. She doesn't get mad if her sister has something that she doesn't have. There's a purity in her emotional and mental makeup that is different from most other children. Most kids want to interact with her, given the opportunity.

There is something magical about her that draws people to her, both adults and children. Maybe that magic helps to balance out what she's missing.

MOM: Sometimes you almost think the world would be a better place if there were more people like Parisa.

— FOURTEEN TO SEVENTEEN YEARS —

In some ways, for us it's easier now that she and her brother are older and we have a better idea of who they're going to be. When they are two, when they are three, you don't know if you have a child that's going to be independent some day or not. You don't know if you have a child that's going to be able to have their own family some day or not. But then you get to a point, when they're a certain age, that you have a pretty good idea of where they're going. And, you deal with that. In some ways, it becomes easier, because you have a path. Even if the path isn't the original one you thought you had, you can finally look toward the future. When she was younger I would usually think in terms of six months ahead, when trying to track her future development. Now, I can look a few years ahead. We have more of an idea of who she is.

– *Esther's mom*

Everything changes. It's dynamic. She's already progressed past the point where I thought she'd ever get so I'm always optimistic about her. I respect her and I'm just amazed by her. I know she has rough days at school, but she's a little soldier. She gets through a lot of stuff amazingly.

– *Christina's dad*

I never had patience, and she has taught me to have patience. I needed to stop and smell the flowers. You just take one day at a time. Sometimes, I think it would be great if we all lived in Joy's world. Her world is so much better than ours. She thinks everybody is good. She's always happy.

– *Joy's mom*

—ESTHER —

14 YEARS | 5 MONTHS

Sarah (younger sister) and Esther

Esther can tell when people are teasing her meanly, and she doesn't
like it. She will ignore them completely... The ones who are nice to her
all the time, she sees them. She will smile back and say hi.

Esther's mom

What would you like to tell me about Esther?

MOM: Esther is very sweet and loving. One of her strong points is her gentle nature. She doesn't get mad or frustrated easily. Believe me; I would get frustrated a lot if I had her challenges. Essie has been working very hard and she's learned a lot of things. She is good at cooperating and she can be helpful. Although Esther is completely nonverbal, she understands a lot. Essie likes being with people. She remembers people and she can tell when people are being nice to her. She also remembers when people are not nice to her.

It does get better. Some of it is you adjusting. But over time they adjust as well. She used to be very shy. She loved people that she knew, but took longer to warm up to strangers. Now, if someone's nice to her, she warms up right away. Esther can tell when people are teasing her meanly, and she doesn't like it. She will ignore them completely. She'll treat them like furniture. And she does not normally treat people like furniture. She doesn't get angry, but for her they're just not there. And if later they try to say hello to her nicely, because an authority figure is watching, she still doesn't see them. The ones who are nice to her all the time, she sees them. She will smile back and say hi.

What are Essie's favorite things to do?

MOM: She loves school. She's going to be in high school next year. She's the one child in the family that's always happy to get on the bus. She loves going to plays and she loves watching the circus. We took to her to Las Vegas once and there were some acrobats performing out on the street. Most people were walking by. Essie watched and clapped. They ended up performing just for Essie. They all bowed to her. She does love a performance.

She likes riding in the car. She likes riding on the bus. She likes traveling. She loves vacations and staying in hotels and getting to sleep in a great big bed with Mommy and her sister. She loves being in the pool. She loves water play. She likes the beach and any kind of water. She loves the aquarium.

She likes our dog, Goldie. She sneaks food under the table for the dog. She's the only one who does. No one else is allowed. Her older brother, who is also autistic, wouldn't and her younger brother and sister know that they're not allowed. Essie is allowed, because everyone is happy that she understands that the dog is begging.

When they were young, everyone was saying that the brain is developing, and the windows of opportunity are closing, and you've got to do this now, and you've got to do that now, and you've got to press hard. We did a lot of it. But we never did beyond the point where the family seemed not like a loving family. She had occupational therapy. She had speech therapy. She had the school based ABA program. At home we privately hired some college students to come and play with her and keep her motivated and engaged after school. But, we didn't have an official protocol that they had to teach her. We had them follow her lead, and just play with her and interact. She loved it. It was more like the Floortime/DIR model. It worked for her. It so depends on the child. My son did well with ABA. He learned a lot of skills that way. But, for Esther, it was not appropriate. Every kid is different.

Esther is happy. She's had a happy childhood and we have a happy family. Our marriage is strong. We're partners and we're happy together. The pressure on parents of autistic kids when they are first diagnosed is so hard and there are so many choices to make so quickly and so many people willing to take your money, and take your time. You need to just relax and be a family and love your kid, and give yourself the right to live and be a mom.

What else would you like to tell someone whose child just received a diagnosis of ASD.
MOM: To someone who suspects a problem, but doesn't yet have a diagnosis, I would absolutely recommend that they get their child checked immediately. If you have any suspicions, you want to go to someone who is an expert in autism, and you want to go as quickly as possible.

– ESTHER –

To someone who has the diagnosis, don't look back. It's so pointless. Some parents carry lots of guilt because someone told them that they should have received therapy sooner. First of all, it's probably not at all true. You have a child. You love that child. Do what's best for them now. Don't worry about the past.

Obviously, doing nothing is not going to help any child. I think that there's a certain amount of potential that's going to be there, no matter what therapies you pursue. Some of these kids are going to be disabled their whole lives, no matter what you do. They're still wonderful people. You want to help them reach their full potential, like you would with any child. And you want them to feel loved and appreciated for who they are. Even those who are going to be able to make it to higher levels should be appreciated all along the way and not feel that they're not important or that they're not cherished for who they are right now. Every child deserves that. You love and accept your child no matter what.

In some ways, for us it's easier now that she and her brother are older and we have a better idea of who they're going to be. When they are two, when they are three, you don't know if you have a child that's going to be independent some day or not. You don't know if you have a child that's going to be able to have their own family some day or not. But then you get to a point, when they're a certain age, that you have a pretty good idea of where they're going. And, you deal with that. In some ways, it becomes easier, because you have a path. Even if the path isn't the original one you thought you had, you can finally look toward the future. When she was younger I would usually think in terms of six months ahead, when trying to track her future development. Now, I can look a few years ahead. We have more of an idea of who she is.

— ADAM —

14 YEARS | 7 MONTHS

Everybody is different ...
We're just different in our own special ways.

Adam

How would you describe Adam?

MOM: I would describe Adam as very laid-back. He's very well-behaved with us. He's a really nice teenager.

DAD: He's good-natured. He has a good heart. He has empathy for other kids, especially kids that are getting picked on.

MOM: He's super-intelligent, super-creative, and just a super kid. We never could complain about him when he was growing up because he never caused us problems. It was only when he was with kids that you noticed this social withdrawal. He didn't know how to interact with kids.

Now he has lots of friends. They are mostly kids that have unique characteristics. I've never seen his friends being judgmental, like teenagers can be. I've never seen Adam pass judgment. If anything, Adam is the first to say, "Give him or her an opportunity. Don't pass judgment." He actually keeps me, as a mother, in check.

We're lucky because our town is a very small art community. The kids are exposed to a lot of the arts growing up, so many of them are very creative including Adam. Kids used to attend the local talent shows because they knew that Adam and his friends were going to be onstage. His music teacher says that Adam has perfect pitch, and is gifted. Adam has also been featured in town because of his autism. He's been accepted as a special part of the community.

DAD: His music teacher is excited about what Adam is doing with guitar. He said that Adam picks up very quickly, is really motivated and innovative. This is a kid who had to be taught how to hold a pencil. Now can play the guitar really well.

MOM: Until he was probably about ten-years-old, he would make noises and stim with his fingers and hands. We'd make him aware of what he was doing, though we understood why he was doing it. If he was behaving in ways that weren't socially appropriate, we would always give him other behavioral options. Rather than trying to end the behavior, if he was being irritated by sounds, he could tap instead of making noises. We'd give him a squishy ball that he kept in his pocket to use instead of stimming with his hands. We never said that he wasn't allowed to do something, because we knew he had to. That's what we learned in OT. She taught us that it's okay to substitute behaviors versus completely eradicating them. As a parent, that was very valuable advice.

DAD: It was harder when he was younger because at parties he would get overwhelmed and over-stimulated. Also, he was a little hyper and a little demanding.

MOM: When Adam first got diagnosed we were very concerned. That was before we knew how much OT using sensory integration would help him. Today there are so many more options. There is so much more optimism than there was ten years ago.

When Adam was eleven or twelve-years-old he was being bullied for a brief time. It was a little intimidating for him. We all get bullied. We have all been rejected. That's a painful lesson of childhood. But the difference with Adam is that being bullied didn't sink in and take hold like it does with so many other kids. It didn't define who Adam was. It didn't rule his life. Adam wasn't afraid to get on the bus. He didn't like it, but he was never afraid of it. Finally he went in by himself and met with the principal. He got a restraining order which said that the bully had to stay at least twenty feet away from him. He felt empowered enough to go by himself to the principal. And it worked. That's another thing that we love about Adam. Growing up he was always able to say, "This feels uncomfortable, so I'm not going to do it that way. I'm going to do it my way."

Is there anything that you'd like to tell other parents?

MOM: I want to tell parents not to panic. I want parents to know that it's not the end of the world. I want them to know that there's help at any stage.

DAD: If they get their child in therapy, no matter what level they're at, they'll improve. How dramatically? It's hard to know. But you'll never know what their potential is if you do nothing. It's not a death knell. It's a beginning. And then you have to take action for them…

MOM: … despite your own fears or concerns. Every parent goes through a range of emotions when they find out that their child is different from other kids. We didn't know how Adam was going to turn out.

DAD: It's a fear of the unknown. It's important to be proactive as a parent and not be afraid of a label. And it's important to not be in denial. Parents have to put their kid ahead of their own feelings and ahead of any fear of being rejected by society. It's also important to lighten up, if possible, because it can get pretty heavy dealing with all of it.

Adam, how would you describe autism?

ADAM: I would describe it as sort of a gift. It makes you really special in a lot of ways. I have hyper-senses, so I can see words that are really tiny from really far away. My friends will point to something far away and ask, "What does that say?" And I'll be able to tell them. I can also hear things, like when the dog gets all whiney in another room or something, I can hear him.

Everybody is different. Your autism doesn't affect you. It doesn't make you different from anybody else: "Oh, let's avoid him because he's autistic." We're just the same as everybody else. We're just different in our own special ways.

If you could, is there anything you'd want to change about your life?

ADAM: Nothing. There is nothing I wish was different about me. I like me just the way I am. Are there things that bother me? Nothing that I have a break down over, nothing that drives me insane.

MOM: Adam, what do you want to do with your life?

ADAM: Anything that will help kids. I want to make a difference in the understanding of autism.

— CHRISTINA —
14 YEARS | 6 MONTHS

Brittany (older sister) and Christina

Just take one step at a time. And when you
have a bad day, just go with the flow.
Christina

– CHRISTINA –

How would you describe Christina?

DAD: Christina is a ball of energy.

MOM: She has a wonderful sense of humor. It's so funny and unexpected. She's very observant. Sometimes it takes a while before the humor comes out. But when it does it just cracks you up, because it's so deep.

BRITTANY: And she can be a little peacemaker. One time my dad, myself and my mom were arguing over some teenage angst-y thing. All of a sudden, in the middle of it all, I hear this little voice singing, "and I think to myself what a wonderful world..." We all started laughing because she had just nailed it.

MOM: Her sister is very important to her. In the past she would do something because Brittany did it. She would do it even if she didn't like it because Brittany did it. But now, she's more able to do things that she, Christina, wants to do. Although it's difficult for her to keep up with other kids in some things, she can keep up in outdoor activities. The more outdoor things she does the happier she is.

DAD: She likes fishing and hiking. She's a little mountain goat.

CHRISTINA: And swimming, since I was six.

MOM: There were a lot more concerns in her younger years. She was always falling down. Sometimes she would be up on her toes. Her OT and PT recommended a lot of balance activities and weighted things. Carrying weight helped her know where her body was.

DAD: When she watched T.V., if she got visually locked in, she wouldn't know where her body was and just fall over.

MOM: Christina likes to perform. She can stand up in front of a whole church. She's a very good altar server. She knows when the priest needs something. When something occasionally goes wrong, she's able to adapt and take care of it. She's good with the younger ones, keeping them quiet, and guiding them with what to do, in a very quiet, very kind way.

DAD: There have been times when she was the only one that showed up. She did a wedding all by herself.

MOM: On the other hand, Christina is working on being more flexible in daily life. If we say that we're going to leave in ten minutes, but don't leave for thirty minutes, she gets anxious. Or it bothers her if we change the restaurant we're going to. She's working on being flexible when things have to change.

Christina is also still working on her social skills. At school, at recess or lunch Christina will often be all by herself. It's hard work catching the typical social signals that maybe the other kids pick up on. And then, sometimes she just doesn't care and she doesn't want to have to do it. She doesn't understand why the other girls might walk off when she says something random, or why she's not included in something, or why she might get in trouble for doing something impulsive. She's perplexed. But Christina is learning to stick in there more socially. There are good times and not so good times. Also, self-care used to be a real struggle. Now she sorts her own clothes and she can do the laundry.

DAD: She does the dishes and can cook some of her own food.

MOM: She can do her room really neat if she sets her mind to it. The big thing now is that she's responsible for her planner and for doing her homework. I didn't think that would ever happen. There used to be a struggle because we always had to monitor her and she wanted us out of her business since she's a teenager. It was that way for a couple of years. Now she sits down and does her homework and she's very thorough, for the most part. If there's something that's really hard or she doesn't understand then she will let it go. It's not a perfect thing. But for her to sit down and do what she's been doing recently is incredible. With some things it can take years. You think, "We should have been over this by now." But you just keep doing it. You keep doing a little bit of exposure here and there and you just don't give up. No matter how badly it turns out, you just keep doing it. Because that's how she progresses.

DAD: Everything changes. It's dynamic. She's already progressed past the point where I thought she'd ever get so I'm always optimistic about her. I respect her and I'm just amazed by her. I know she has rough days at school, but she's a little soldier. She gets through a lot of stuff amazingly.

CHRISTINA: I usually just don't mention it.

LINDA: For a long time now Christina has told people, "My brain works different."

CHRISTINA: Yeah, because I think I use math differently, and I can't write words correct when my teacher says it and they get somebody else to write down the words.

MOM: To take notes for her.

Christina, if another fourteen-year old had unique ways of doing things, like you do, is there anything you'd like to tell her?

CHRISTINA: Just take one step at a time. And when you have a bad day, just go with the flow.

Brittany, what would you like to say to the kids out there?

BRITTANY: I would say just because they're different there's nothing wrong with them. They belong, they have a purpose, and they're all beautiful people that have special traits. Every one of them has value, and, to never forget that. And to always believe in themselves because they have a purpose and a place in the world.

CHRISTINA: Well, said! You should give a speech on that, Brittany.

BRITTANY: To the moms and dads, I realize that it can never be easy to raise a child who is developing differently and is seen as different by everyone else. But, it's worth it and the love that that kid will have for you, for the support that you give them, is a very important gift.

— JOY —

15 YEARS | 6 MONTHS

Sometimes, I think it would be great if we all lived in Joy's world.
Her world is so much better than ours. She thinks everybody is
good. She's always happy.

Joy's mom

When someone hears the term autism they can sometimes have preconceived notions. What would you like them to know about your daughter?

MOM: I always tell people about Joy's diagnosis. But I also say that if you meet her you would never know. She's like any other kid. She rides horses. She's in choir. She's a phenomenal student. She is unbelievably creative and imaginative. She's always in a good mood and joyous. I call it "Joy's World." She's an avid reader. I say that she's recovered. She still has some OCD[22] issues, which might be related to autism, but she's gotten so much better with those issues.

How are her social skills?

MOM: Her social skills are good now. When she was little they were horrible. Now she has some friends at school, but she never makes plans for the weekends. Making plans is out of her comfort zone. I think it bothers me more than it bothers her. I think she's more comfortable being alone than I am. Socially she's not your typical teenager. But on the other hand if she was a typical teenager I'd have to worry about her going out at night, or running with boys, or on the phone until two in the morning. That's your typical teenager nowadays. Which one would I rather have? I'd much rather have this one.

How did her diagnosis come about?

MOM: She was diagnosed when she was about two and half. I always knew something was wrong. She would be stimming all the time. Once she started walking, she was always on her tippy toes. Otherwise, she was mostly developing normally. But, she never really developed language. I think the words were probably in her head but she couldn't get them to come out. In kindergarten she started talking more. It was like a cloud had lifted. She has always been sensitive to some things, like noisy places. And she can't stand the feeling of certain material, but it's not horrible. Everyone has things they like and things they don't. She's just a little bit more particular.

---

22   Obsessive-Compulsive Disorder

When your child is first diagnosed you go through the grieving process because the child that you thought you had is no longer there. Now a new child is born. As tough as it's been I would never trade it. In fact, she has taught me. I was so type A. I truly believe in fate. I believe it was God's way of telling me that I have to slow down and cool it, and this kid is going to show me the path. I never had patience, and she has taught me to have patience. I needed to stop and smell the flowers. You just take one day at a time. Sometimes, I think it would be great if we all lived in Joy's world. Her world is so much better than ours. She thinks everybody is good. She's always happy.

JOY: On social media I put, "I reject reality and make my own." I've been horseback riding for about four years. I also love comics. I think that compared to other people I have a more creative mind. What I really like doing is cartooning. There's this whole process to drawing cartoons.

How would you describe autism, if someone asked you about it?

JOY: I don't know if there are actually things that I can point to that make me feel autistic. What does it feel like to be non-autistic? My definition of autism? I've never really thought about a definition for autism. It's something that you're born with. There are all levels of autism, with different capacities. And, there are different types, like Asperger's. Whenever I see autism in movies, it seems like they over-act. When people hear about autism they think it means the child is mentally delayed or mentally disabled. They think that the child can't do anything. My friends don't really know that I have autism. I would tell them if it came up. They would probably be surprised.

There will be times when my head will feel kind of, not really empty, just kind of nervous in a way. But I don't really know why. I think that's only if I'm stressed out or something. I will start fiddling with my hands and I will kind of scrunch up.

Does that help you feel better?

JOY: Yeah. Sometimes my head just feels kind of on overload. When I was little I really didn't like the noise of a flushing toilet. I really didn't like the sound of fingernails across some kinds of plastic. It would give me the chills. Now it's not that bad. I was at a Bat Mitzvah and it was really loud, but I didn't really mind. I got used to it. But at homecoming I was a little uncomfortable because I went by myself. It was really loud. I couldn't hear myself. I couldn't hear anybody else. That was just annoying.

I think I daydream a lot more as compared to most people. Sometimes pulling the ends of my hair helps me daydream more because then I'm not focusing on anything else. When I'm in the car, if I'm not sleeping, I'm daydreaming. Sometimes I'll think of certain music, and I'll create a scene with background music in it. I write poetry and songs and I draw. I wrote a poem called "Feel." It's not at all how I actually feel, because it sounds like I'm really depressed. It's not actually how I feel. I wrote it at camp last summer. I was just sitting there and it came to me.

FEEL
Ever feel that the greatest decision you've made was for the worst,
Or that a team play you made was good for you, but not everyone else?
Or maybe the person who tells you everything was actually a lie?
Ever feel yourself getting smaller every day,
Or significantly shrinking as you see people rise around you,
Or the numb-pounding feeling in your heart telling you that they're not coming back?
Ever feel that you wish you could feel nothing, no pain, mentally and physically,
So you can never get hurt again?
But if you cannot ever feel these feelings,
How is one supposed to know all the good feelings if you can't feel the bad?
How are we supposed to feel pain if we can't feel at all?
Pain is an essential need. No matter how much it hurts, we need it.
We have it. So don't ignore it. Follow it to a better path of happiness.

— ANDREW —
15 YEARS | 8 MONTHS

He says he wants to be a game show host. He has a very vibrant, bubbly
personality. You never know. But then, as any parent would do, you ask,
"What's the back-up career?"

Andrew's dad

– ANDREW –

How would you describe Andrew?

MOM: Andrew is very endearing to people. He's a good kid.

DAD: He is very happy. Andrew is very unassuming and not afraid to talk to anyone. We often hear, "You have a very charming son." He has a positive outlook on everything. Members of our temple often comment about his Bar Mitzvah, saying how comfortable and natural he appeared throughout it. They could see that he really enjoyed the whole thing. In a way it was like a performance. He enjoys having the spotlight.

MOM: It's not that he did any better than any of the other kids. It was just the way he presented himself. Andrew also gave a speech when the temple honored us as a couple.

DAD: He had everybody in stitches. He stole the show, as usual. At one point he was reading his speech, with help from an adult. He added a few impromptu remarks, including mentioning something about autism, and then he paused, and said, "I'm glad I have autism" and just kept reading his speech. Some of the adults said that was the best moment of the night. Andrew knows he has autism and that he thinks differently. That's his definition of autism "thinking differently." He's been diagnosed with both high-functioning autism and Asperger's.

MOM: It depends on who you ask. It can be hard for children and teens on the autism spectrum to live in this world. Either the lights bother them or whatever. Andrew doesn't like loud noises. He hates balloons because they might pop.

DAD: He hates the Fourth of July. This last Fourth of July, he locked himself in the bathroom for a couple hours with his video games and he was fine.

MOM: There are no windows and he had the fan on.

DAD: It was worse when he was younger.

MOM: We were in an elevator and somebody was chewing gum and popped a bubble. It was loud, and he didn't like it.

DAD: From then on he connected gum with that loud sound, so he would get upset when he saw someone chewing gum.

MOM: He used to hate the sound of the vacuum. He would run from the room screaming if the door to the downstairs closet was opened because that's where the vacuum cleaner is stored.

DAD: Now, although he doesn't like the sound of the vacuum cleaner, he can deal with it. He just covers his ears and asks, "When are you going to be done?"

How is he doing in school?

MOM: Andrew is finishing his freshman year.

DAD: He's on a diploma track in high school, so he'll receive a regular diploma rather than just receiving a certificate. He's never had his curriculum modified. He's always been in a regular classroom. He's not the problem kid in class. He's the one who conforms and does what he's supposed to do.

MOM: He has resource lab. That's the only support he gets and that's all he needs.

DAD: Abstract concepts are challenging. His strength is in things that he can memorize. And we're working on his reading comprehension. After he sees a movie, he has trouble summarizing it for someone else. He can tell you certain plot points but nothing subtle and nothing that would really connect it all together very well and has trouble sequencing the story. He has difficulty writing an essay that is really thoughtful and sequential and has meaning.

MOM: He doesn't get the big picture.

Does he have friends at school?

DAD: He doesn't really have any close friends at school. He just enjoys talking to people. He'll walk up to someone, introduce himself, and have a very limited conversation or just tell them facts. He doesn't really care about having a sustained conversation. He likes talking to people, being with people, but not really interacting in a hugely meaningful way.

MOM: You would imagine that he would get upset because he doesn't fit in, but he doesn't mind. For him it is not a big deal. He does his own thing and he is happy doing whatever he is doing.

DAD: Some kids do laugh at him, because he is a little different and quirky. But there are others who can see beyond that. He doesn't have any social pretense. He'll get up in front of the crowd and just start dancing. It's the kind of thing most kids wouldn't do. He doesn't care if he looks goofy or different. And if people were to make fun of him, he probably wouldn't get it. The fact that he doesn't get upset usually stops them. They are usually just trying to get a rise out of him, but he is not going to understand or care. Eventually, they're like "whatever." He just wants to do his own thing and is just fine by himself. It's more difficult for us because we're used to being social, having friends, and looking forward to being invited to events. He doesn't care, except that he wants to be invited so he can go places and be among people.

What are your hopes for him?

MOM: Our hope for him is that he can live on his own.

DAD: He says he wants to be a game show host. He has a very vibrant, bubbly personality. You never know. But then, as any parent would do, you ask, "What's the back-up career?" We have talked with him about it and he suggested that he might be an accountant, which is great because he loves math and he's very good with numbers. So that might be a bit more practical and realistic for him. He'll figure it out.

— BRITTANY —
15 YEARS | 5 MONTHS

I would describe Brittany as tentative, a little shy, and quiet. She takes her time... She appreciates other people and gives a lot of compliments. To her, every girl is beautiful and a princess.

Brittany's mom

When were your three children diagnosed?

MOM: Brittany's older brother was about nine. Brittany was probably five or six, and Amberly[23] was around three. Brittany actually talked right on time. Then at about two and a half years old she stopped progressing and regressed a bit. She just kind of plateaued for a long time. Finally, she started making real progress again around fourth grade.

We had been concerned about all three of our kids. Eventually, when we did an autism rating scale, I started to see the whole picture. Finally I had a starting point. We called the local university, which has a specialized program for autism, and set up evaluations. It took a long time to get in, because they had a long waiting list. The diagnosis was autism for all three of them, but our son has high-functioning autism. There was a lot of stuff to read. I read and read and read and read and then I got to the point where I had to back away. I had to stop. And we got them into therapies. They are still receiving OT at a local clinic, and they've received speech therapy as well. I had finally got my questions answered, but on the other hand I got a big load.

How would you describe Brittany?

MOM: I would describe Brittany as tentative, a little shy and quiet. She takes her time. She is very loving, kind, and thoughtful of other people. She loves her sister and her brother. She tolerates physical affection. She appreciates other people and gives a lot of compliments. To her, every girl is beautiful and a princess. She's very nice.

Brittany is also sensitive to any criticism. We have to be very gentle when correcting her. We try to always use a positive redirection and stay away from negative words and attitudes. Brittany internalizes things more than her brother and sister. She'll cry about things, like the death of an

---

23 Amberly, page 168

animal. She worries and is concerned about her little sister. But she's bossy with her older brother. She can be bossy with a lot of people. There's a little boy in her class who has severe autism. Brittany acts like a little mom with him. The teacher often tells him, "Calm body." Now Brittany will say that to him as well and he'll listen to Brittany. She has her bossy moments. But, she's mostly a sweetheart.

Brittany is rarely harsh or unkind to other people. She's mostly very gentle. She could easily be taken advantage of because of it. She has no desire to get ahead or to do things better than other people. She's not competitive. She doesn't care about having the prettiest clothes and that kind of thing.

She's very pure in her way of thinking. Not that she's perfect. She has her moments. But, mostly, she's nice. Family things are really important to Brittany. She also loves babies. She was really fascinated when I was nursing her little sister. She was very into how babies are born and things having to do with babies and homemaking.

What are Brittany's favorite things to do?
MOM: Brittany likes to cook. She has a chef's hat and an apron and some kid's books on cooking. And she's an artist. She is good at sewing and drawing and art in general. She is good with her hands. She's better at puzzles than most people. Brittany's favorite thing to do is to draw pictures of princesses and make up stories. She'll make an illustrated version of a story. She'll draw page after page and then make up a story with a few captions here and there.

Does Brittany enjoy school?
MOM: She has mixed emotions about school. In the morning, she doesn't like it too much. When she gets home, she says it was great. I think she has anxiety about transitions. For her the transition to high school is going to be tricky. I might drive her over for the first few weeks, and have her arrive late. That way she won't have the "wake up earlier" thing and the bus thing and the new school thing all at the same time. We transition her into all the changes a little at a time.

– BRITTANY –

Brittany's in a self-contained special needs class. Her best subject is reading. Brittany was the only one in her class who could read with inflection. She's reading at about fourth or fifth grade level. She has some comprehension.

Brittany has had the same core friends in her class that she's had for a while. She hasn't really branched out. She likes the other kids but she doesn't talk much about them. She needs prompting to interact. Her best friend moved away in fourth or fifth grade. Brittany was not at all emotional about it. She told me that her friend was moving to a pink house. That was about all.

People really don't know what autism is and have misunderstandings about kids with autism. It doesn't mean that they aren't individuals. They can do a lot of things. Maybe they can't do all the things you had hoped they could do. But they can do a lot of happy, fun things. My kids are mostly happy. They enjoy their life. They don't mind. They don't know what they should be able to do. They're fine.

— DAVID —

16 YEARS | 9 MONTHS

If you go to another country and you don't speak the language it can be
very frustrating trying to get yourself understood. And, David is trying.
He is putting out three hundred times the effort compared to what
we're putting out for him. He's an amazing kid.

David's mom

– DAVID –

How would you describe David's personality?

MOM: David is very sweet, loving, and caring. He's also very sensitive

DAD: He wants to please in the worst way. You ask him to go change a tire in a car or rebuild the engine, he'll be out there. He won't know how to do it, but he'll be trying to do what you ask.

MOM: He will be completely frustrated if he can't please you. He's also very patient. Considering all that this child has been through, all the medical tests, all the assessments, all the inept educational programming that he's endured, the fact that's he's not abusive or aggressive and that he's still so complacent, wants to please and willing to do whatever we ask of him, is amazing. There aren't many people who could endure all of that probing and not get angry or bitter or whatever. There are times when he would have every right to scream, "Why aren't you getting that I don't know what you're saying? Help me!" If you go to another country and you don't speak the language it can be very frustrating trying to get yourself understood. And, David is trying. He is putting out three hundred times the effort compared to what we're putting out for him. He's an amazing kid.

DAD: In junior high it was really clear that he wanted to be like other kids and do what the other kids did. It totally surprised us. You think that he's not aware of his surroundings. But, somewhere in there, he is very much aware. It would be great if we could tap into what's in there. He wanted to wear the kind of clothes that the other kids are wearing and things like that.

MOM: When he goes to his therapies he looks for age-appropriate toys and activities to do. He doesn't obsess on the younger kids toys. They don't interest him. He looks for things that are definitely more age-appropriate. He likes to help cook. He loves doing jigsaw puzzles. He likes word search puzzles. He really enjoys going fishing with his dad.

DAD: We'll go out on the boat or there's a pond down the street.

MOM: He likes the water and playing in the pool. He loves campfires.

Are there things that bother him?

MOM: His hearing has always been very sensitive. We've have to make sure he sees the vacuum before turning it on.

He also used to be really bothered if a container was partially filled. If the hand soap was half empty, he'd pump it until it was gone. The furniture in the living room got trashed because he poured corn oil over it.

DAD: Even when he would pour something into a glass, if there was a little left in the container, he'd pour it until it was gone and overflow the glass.

He seems to understand a lot more than he can express. Is that right?

MOM: Yes. He has functional communication. He can tell me something he needs or he wants. David has a combination of verbal apraxia and word finding problems, so his speech is very difficult to understand, sometimes even with familiar listeners. He has a communication device, which we're learning to use. He's a visual learner. Once something is presented to him in a visual format, he gets it and he's usually able to follow through. David has functional communication. He can tell us if he needs or wants something.

DAD: But he won't initiate conversation just for the sake of conversation.

MOM: And just because he can't talk doesn't mean that he's not intelligent. He understands phonics and can decode words. He reads at about a third grade level. His fine motor is not great for handwriting. We still struggle with that. He can write some. He can sign his name. He's independent in dressing himself and brushing his teeth and with most daily living skills. He'll be starting his senior year in high school.

For David, having it written out is very helpful. If it's not written, and you didn't understand what he said, and you repeat back something different to him, he thinks he said the wrong thing to you. So he'll pick another word, because, he wants to please you. If he asks for something and you say, "David, I didn't hear you," he'll say something different. He's thinking, "That's not what she wanted me to say, so I'd better say this." It works better if we write it down for him. One of the hardest things for us is that he can't spontaneously tell us things. If he has a medical problem and it comes on slowly David acclimates to it.

DAD: And if we ask him "Does it hurt?" or, "Where does it hurt?" he can't tell us.

MOM: We've been very fortunate because a lot of people who have worked with David know that he's a great kid. And people in the community are very accepting. When David was younger, he'd be so quick that he'd be down at the road before we knew. A neighbor would call, "Do you know that David's down here?" People recognized him and were very understanding and supportive of us.

DAD: Kids in the community have been great to him. When we take him shopping, kids will come up and say, "Hi, David!" And, then I'll say, "Well, Dave, are you going to say hi?" And, he'll usually say hi. David was the guest speaker for a national fund-raiser.

MOM: It was the organization that provided the funding for David's communication device. He presented a little speech about what having the device has meant to him. He read part of it. Then we had the rest of the speech programmed into his device so that he just had to push a button. It was in front of about three hundred and fifty people. He did great. We thought that the noise would be too much for him. Everybody gave him a standing ovation, of course. And, he was fine. Afterwards, people came up to him and he got it. He stood up, shook hands, and said, "Hi, I'm David." It was a big to-do. It was pretty cool.

— ARIEL —

17 YEARS | 8 MONTHS

I like to read... Right now I'm reading *Wuthering Heights*... After
high school I want to try to become a marine biologist.

Ariel

− ARIEL −

How would you describe your daughter?

MOM: Ariel is very kind and generous. She has a big heart. She's just a great girl. In retrospect, I would say she was always a little bit different, a little bit special. She didn't get diagnosed till she was older, because she behaves nicely. She didn't talk very much. People just thought she was shy. She would sit quietly and not make any disturbances.

She is in regular classes. She doesn't need any extra help. School goes pretty well. Her grades are usually A's, B's. Every once in a while she'll get overwhelmed and just stop doing her homework. Then she has to make up for it and that's hard. She likes to do well so most of the time she tries to get everything done. She's still working on asking for help when she gets stuck. She doesn't like to tell people that she's struggling. Even though I keep telling her that everybody struggles, everybody needs help. She doesn't like to bother people.

Ariel doesn't like crowds and loud noises. Lunch in middle and high school was difficult until she found teachers that would let her eat her lunch in their classroom where it was quiet. She can usually figure out ways to adapt situations that are hard for her. In elementary school recess was stressful. They would let her work in the office where it was quiet. She would file and help out.

When she was younger we'd go to the mall and she'd only be able to be there for a little while before she'd get really over-stimulated. I think that she would get bothered a little bit by all the visual, but it was mostly the noise. Her hearing is very good. She can hear everything. Although, sometimes she does better with background noise. She actually does better doing her homework with the TV on. And ever since she was little, you couldn't disrupt her routine or it really messed her up.

Even when she was a little baby she didn't like too much stimulation. We had one of those baby slings. Her two sisters were always trying to look out, but she didn't want to look out. She wanted to be covered and only look in. But as long as we carried her, she never cried, so she was a very easy baby. She was always super sensitive to lights and sounds.

When she was little and the kids would go out to play, she'd sit by herself in the corner by the tree or she'd stand at the edge of the group of girls. She really didn't know how to approach them. She's gotten better over the years. It's very difficult as a parent to teach something that is second nature for the rest of us. When she was younger she did have friends, but sometimes she'd still just sit by herself over by the tree, and wouldn't play with the other girls. It looked like it was hard for her to figure out how to join in a game.

What would you say are Ariel's strengths?

MOM: I admire that she tries to push herself to do things that are not comfortable for her. We had a German exchange student last year. Ariel was fine with having the girl here, but I know she pushed herself hard to go to all the parties and all the events so that the girl would feel comfortable going too. Normally Ariel would not have wanted to go to all those events.

When she was sixteen she went to Germany for a month and lived with the family of the girl who had been with us. It was really hard on her, because it was such a big change and it was very difficult. Our older daughter went over as well, so Ariel would have someone who knew her and could help if needed.

We're working on learning how to drive and those kinds of things. It's a little scary. That's where all those motor skills come in that she's been developing. One of her strengths is that she's very organized. She's smart. She is very responsible about things that she takes on. She loves animals and she always will do the very best she can to take care of them.

Each child is an individual and every child's abilities, whether they have autism or not, are individual. They should not be lumped into one big category. Everybody needs to be treated as an individual with their own strengths and weaknesses, like all of us have.

ARIEL: Autism has certain aspects of ADHD[24]. I can't focus on one thing for too long. Sometimes when I look at something for too long, my eyes will actually sort of hurt. And I can't stay sitting still for too long. I can't do one thing for too long. I like to move around and break it up.

---

24   ADHD: Attention Deficit Hyperactivity Disorder

What are your favorite things to do?

ARIEL: I like to read, and watch TV shows or movies. Right now I'm reading *Wuthering Heights*.

How old where you when you started riding horses?

ARIEL: Ten. I try to come once a week at least.

Are there things that you are still learning to do?

ARIEL: I have to work on coming out and talking to people.

Is that something you want to do?

ARIEL: Yeah. Usually, I'm the one who starts off with conversations and stuff. It takes a while, but usually it's me. I'm shy with new people, but I can get pretty outgoing with my friends.

What are your plans for after high school?

ARIEL: After high school I want to try to become a marine biologist and maybe like work in behind the scenes animal care at Sea World. I went to a camp at Sea World a couple times, when I was fourteen or fifteen. We got to see where they had the rescued animals and the pregnant animals. We got to help the people who make the food and train the animals. I liked that.

MOM: Is there anything else that you want to tell Shay?

ARIEL: I think the old saying says it best, "Don't judge a book by its cover."

Because they could miss the wonderful thing that's inside, right? Like you.

ARIEL: Me

— EPILOGUE —

While there are societal norms to which individuals on the spectrum are compared and expected to fit within, more needs to be done to honor and nurture who they are, to empower them and help them become their own self-advocates. As one mother said, "This is fun for us to get a chance to brag about our son. We don't often get that opportunity. There's so much information about the problems of autism, and there is definitely a time and a place for that. But I'm glad that we also get to share what is wonderful about our son."

This book is dedicated to the parents as they navigate the steep learning curve that accompanies their child's diagnosis of autism spectrum disorder. It is for their families and friends, who are seeking greater insight into the autism spectrum experience. It is for the professionals who are a part of these lives, to help us all remember to ask for and listen to the stories. And it is for society in general, especially those who are interested in understanding the autism spectrum in a deeper, more relational way.

ANNABELLA - 5 YEARS | 11 MONTHS

— ACKNOWLEDGMENTS —

I would like to express my gratitude and appreciation to all who provided support during this long term project.

First and foremost I owe a huge debt of gratitude to the parents, teens, and children who participated. Without their generosity, this book would not have become a reality.

And I extend special thanks to my dream team who, with their expertise and creativity, smoothed the way: Marcia Breece, production; Judy Robertson, graphic designer; and Sheila Bender, development editor.

I would also like to acknowledge the crucial roles of Lawrene Kovalenko, Holly Holyk, Ann Mitchell, Karen Florek, and Judy Robertson who contributed their time reviewing the text and photos, critiquing the project, and providing encouragement.

And I would like to extend deep gratitude to Shirley and Pat Ryan for providing financial support that helped make this project possible; to Annette Ciketic for coordinating the inaugural gallery exhibit of these photos; to Peggy Lindquist and The Corner Store where I completed much of this book; and to Nancy Scott and Mary O'Maley for their guidance.

Finally, I am grateful to all my friends and family who listened, shared ideas, and supported me over the course of this project. I am blessed to have had so many share in this journey.

CPSIA information can be obtained
at www.ICGtesting.com
Printed in the USA
BVHW090224250919
559224BV00002B/5/P